Unshakable

A Woman In Christ

Copyright 2023 by Rossie Manka

All rights reserved. No part of this book may be reproduced or transmitted in any form or by any means, electronic or mechanical, including photocopying, recording, or by any information storage and retrieval system, without permission in writing from the copyright owner. This work is based on the experiences of individuals. Every effort has been made to ensure the accuracy of the content.*

Bulk orders can be requested at
journey2alignmentcoaching.com

Unshakable: A Woman in Christ

Publishing services provided by FEW International Publications, a division of FEW International Organization, LLC; thefewwomen.com

Publishing Coordinator: Kimberly Joy, Founder of FEW International Publications; thefewwomen.com
Editor: Amy Oaks

Co-Editor: Sue Simpson Bark

Cover Design: Angela Riemer

Interior Layout and Design: Angela Riemer

Bible verses are taken from biblegateway.com ©1995-2017, The Zondervan Corporation. All Rights Reserved.

ISBN-979-8-8692-0252-9

*The names and locations have been changed to honor the privacy of certain individuals in this story wherever that was possible. I acknowledge that these are my personal memories of the events depicted in the book and may be recollected differently by others involved. It is not my intent to cause harm to anyone by sharing my experiences and memories of these events. —Rossie Manka

Table of Contents

ACKNOWLEDGEMENTS 9

INTRODUCTION 17

CHAPTER 1

Distant Memories 19

CHAPTER 2

Roots 23

CHAPTER 3

My Career Journey Begins 29

CHAPTER 4

Resilience 35

CHAPTER 5

Identity 39

CHAPTER 6

Falling Through The Cracks 43

CHAPTER 7

The Last Straw 47

CHAPTER 8
Caving In 51

CHAPTER 9
The Pit 55

CHAPTER 10
Starting Fresh 59

CHAPTER 11
Rage and Rebellion 63

CHAPTER 12
Lucifer 69

CHAPTER 13
Perfect Love. 73

CHAPTER 14
Transition 77

CHAPTER 15
Finding The Light 81

CHAPTER 16
True Growth 85

CHAPTER 17
Mercy And Grace 89

CHAPTER 18
  Big Changes 93

CHAPTER 19
  Back To School 97

CHAPTER 20
  Set Free 103

CHAPTER 21
  God's Gift Mateo 107

CHAPTER 22
  Wisdom And Confidence 113

CHAPTER 23
  Walking Like David 121

CHAPTER 24
  The Journey 127

CHAPTER 25
  The Shift Into My Assignment 133
  COMMUNITY ORGANIZATIONS 145
  COMMUNITY RECOGNITION 150
  ABOUT THE AUTHOR 153
  ABOUT THE PUBLISHER 154

I dedicate this book to my dear children who have seen their mother go from struggle and despair to a life of hope, abundance, and joy.

Acknowledgements

To My Dear Husband: Love You! Look at us now! Look at what the Lord has done. We are set free. We are saved. We are loved by God, a love so deep that one cannot comprehend. We are set apart. And now, with our stories, we can help others.

It's easy to look at the past with regret and shame. But I ask that you don't. We didn't know any better. We walked about in darkness and gave into our fleshly nature. The enemy attacked us and we didn't know how to defend ourselves using God's Word. But I say to you:

For we do not wrestle against flesh and blood, but against principalities, against powers, against the rulers of the darkness of this age, against spiritual hosts of wickedness in the heavenly places. (Ephesians 6:12)

Keep growing, keep pushing, keep holding on to God's promises. For He has so much more for us! For with God nothing is impossible. (Luke 1:37)

Nor do I want you, the reader, to look at our faults (his or mine) with thoughts of shame. *We have overcome and have asked God for forgiveness. He has forgiven us and set us free. For whoever is without sin cast the first stone.* (John 8:7)

To Mom: You fought to raise four daughters and I know it wasn't easy. I know it was years of stress, tears, hard work, and frustration, but you did it. And you never gave up, you never gave up on your little girls, even when everything else was falling apart. You took risks and you were not afraid to start over. You provided for us and cared for our well-being when nothing else made sense.

You did the best you could with what you had. I don't want you to look at yourself as a failure in any way. You truly taught me so much, the ethics of hard work and common sense. Please know I wrote my story to help so many others who may be going through the same thing. This book was meant to be a sign of hope.

Mom, I'm sorry that I lashed out as a teen and went my own way. I can't even imagine the hurt I caused you and I hope that you will forgive me for that. I know we are way over all of this, but just in case this book brings back memories, just know that I truly love you and I can't wait to take the journey together that our future decades hold.

P.S. God loves you and that's the best love you can truly have. XOXO

To Dad: I am so blessed that the Lord restored our relationship. I have seen you go through struggles of your own and know the decades of bondage that you faced. I see that now. But now you are truly living. You are well even in your old age because God has restored your youth and set you free! Those five days in Mexico in 2022 that Maricela and I spent with you felt like ten years that the Lord restored. I felt like a child again as I sat at the breakfast table eating huevos rancheros. When I peeked up, you were staring at me with a smile then quickly looked down. I truly felt like a little girl on Christmas morning with her loving dad giving her the gift of love.

Thanks, Dad, I needed that. Thank You, Abba, You knew.

Auntie Chris: My bold Auntie who has the anointing of God wherever she goes. Thank you for helping me write this book. You are a wise woman of God.

Your hunger for the Lord and his ways are engraved in your heart. Your biggest desire is for people to understand and have the knowledge and tools when digging deep into the Word. You are a teacher of His Word. You have helped me throughout the years to do just that. You have always helped Marilyn, Nancy, Sophia, and me understand the Word, even from childhood. Because of this, we are wise beyond our years. Thank you for that ... I don't know that my walk with God would be as strong as it is now if it hadn't been for you. You literally taught us the book of Revelation when we were young. You're such an obedient servant. I can't wait for you to write your children's book! Your heart is for our children and it shows, so I encourage you to continue that journey.

Love you, Tia.

To My Sisters: As we continue to move forward in life, I look back and am amazed at what we have accomplished despite the many obstacles we faced. I thank God for blessing me with such wonderful and fierce sisters. I couldn't imagine doing life alone all those years ago. We held on to each other through thick and thin and never gave up. We are God's Mighty Warriors — True Soldiers of God.

I can't wait to experience and journey through what God has next for us.

Love you Marilyn, Nancy & Sophia.

To My Family: Aunt Ruby, Aunt Elizabeth, Auntie Chris, Aunt Ruthy (RIH), Mom, Uncle Peter, Uncle David (RIH), Uncle Art (RIH) and Grandma (RIH). I love and cherish you all.

To Momma Kim and FEW: Momma Kim, you are a special gift from God. I am so honored that you are mothering such a beautiful tribe of women, your 11 children, and all those babies that you love so much on your global missions. When you say that you awaken, activate, and accelerate, this is an understatement. You do that and so much more. You watch women blossom, you inspire them, you mother them, you become a friend, you take them under your wing, and I am so honored that I am a part of this. We are the FEW, we are women shaking the ground on which we stand, making lasting impressions all for the glory of God. So thank you, Momma Kim and all the beautiful members and sisters of FEW.

To Beth Stone: Thank you, Beth, for always being kind to our family. I can't tell you how much you inspired me along my growth journey. You always saw the good and potential in me and never told me that I couldn't. I am so blessed to have you in my life and honored that we still get to be a part of each other's lives today. Thank you for playing such a huge role in Anthony's life and for saying YES to being his godmother. Besos.

Lawanda Redmond: My Sister in Christ, you are amazing and I thank God for putting us together in his perfect timing. You are so wise and have the strength of a lion. You always remind me of all the things I must do to keep going. With your inspiration and your push, you have greatly helped me fulfill the call to write and fill the pages of this book. Thank you, dear friend, I know God has such great plans for you, more than you can imagine. Just wait on the Lord, for He is faithful.

Ana & Erica: Dear friends, write your stories and strive for excellence. It is never too late to get things right. It is never too late to aspire for more and turn your dreams into a reality. With God, nothing is impossible.

To the Manjarrez Family: Thank you for always taking me in as your own!

Martha Manjarrez Tovar

In Loving Memory of

A Tribute to Martha Manjarrez Tovar: I am sure you would be proud of the release of this book.

You fought a battle none of us could comprehend. Though we prayed and prayed for you to live and not die, we were heartbroken when you passed.

I sat on my bed and I wept; I wept praying for you the night before you entered into eternal peace.

As I wept, I heard the Lord say, "Be still!" I jerked up instantly, wiped away the tears, and said, "Okay, God." Instantly, I heard Him speak to my heart:

Be still and know that I am God. (Psalm 46:10)

My thoughts are not your thoughts, my ways are not your ways. (Isaiah 55:8)

The next morning on September 9, 2023, you breathed your last breath and you left us to be with the Lord. I was so confused; I thought you were going to live and not die. We spoke life and not death over you for days upon weeks. I questioned God and asked Him, "Why?" He led me to John 21:20, and I knew that our prayers were heard, but God did it His way.

Martha, you are truly living in heaven. You are alive and well, fully restored and with the Lord. We will never know those conversations you had with the Lord. You had an intimate relationship with Him and trusted Him through it all. You fought a good fight and kept the faith to the very end. You are my hero. Heroes are the ones that push and push and push, even through the storms, and you certainly did that. I know you were tired. You can rest now.

Thank you for all the good times, and thank you for always loving me. Give momma Alicia a kiss from Anthony and me, and tell the good Lord I say hello.

Introduction

My journey is that of a woman who overcame years of low self-esteem, fits of anger and self-doubt, and a fearful mind that overemphasized every single thing that I experienced in life. I created elaborate stories of what could go wrong in any situation or circumstance. I had no self-worth, and more importantly, no self-identity.

This is the story of faith, where I recount the infinite ways God has guided me through the toughest, most challenging battles during my three decades on this earth. My journey through life has been much like a prodigal daughter who, after living periods of her life in darkness, returned to a father with loving arms open wide. He rescued me from darkness that took me to the depths of hell and back, revealing unwanted spiritual attacks that tormented me for years.

Years and even decades of preparation did not come easy for me. Times like this are often referred to as the wilderness. And now, this is my story of overcoming it all and becoming a successful woman in the engineering and construction environment, and today, in pursuit of work in ministry and entrepreneurship. I have been awakened, activated, and made new in Christ. He has empowered me to be strong in the face of neglect, abuse, and addiction, and to overcome it all.

But they who wait for the Lord shall renew their strength; they shall mount up with wings like eagles; they shall run and not be weary; they shall walk and not be faint. (Isaiah 40:31)

UNSHAKABLE

I can't even count how many times I have used this verse in my life. It has given me strength time and time again. I tell Him, "Lord, I am weary, Abba, I am tired. Will you help me? Will you be my strength? I need your strength and I need your love. The love like no other, the tender love and care of a father, that heals my wounds and mends my shattered heart."

Life isn't perfect, but He is, and in moments of despair, He is my present help. He truly sends help from the sanctuary. He cares. He cares about every detail of my life and yours. That is what makes our God so so good; He isn't too busy for you or me and He especially counts every tear.

If we continue to hope and renew our strength in the Lord, He will open every door to victory so that we may walk into our true purpose and destiny to live a life of freedom and abundance, even through some of the most unfortunate and dark moments of our lives. If we remain faithful and praise Him even through the midst of the storms, great things can and will come. We will soar with wings like eagles strong, mighty, and equipped, and go to heights we have never imagined. Our faith becomes stronger, we no longer look at the storm with fear, but with power and authority, with faith that makes Jesus marvel.

CHAPTER I

Distant Memories

The first abuse happened at the age of eight. He was the upstairs neighbor and a friend of the family. He lived in the home that I had visited many times when my grandma used to live up there. So, I was always comfortable going upstairs. He was an obnoxiously funny and friendly guy with Shirley Temple kind of curly hair who let my sisters and me run up and down his stairway and into his home. Plus, he gave us treats whenever we wanted.

The house we lived in was an A-frame yellow duplex that sat on the top of a hill on the corner of 6th and Washington in Milwaukee. As a kid in the 90s, I loved playing outside and riding my bike with the neighborhood kids. Sometimes when my mother was asleep, we would get bored. There were no cell phones, cable television, or electronics. We just had the good old outdoors and the nearby community park program that served free lunches. Sometimes, which was often, we would sneak out our window and go to a nearby garden where we would jump the fence, sit in the bushes, and eat the old man's produce. He did catch us a few times, our giggles probably giving us away. But, he would just yell, "Get out of my garden!" Then we would run so fast and get out of there. We were just those kinds of kids, fearless rascals who got into everything.

Well, one day I was alone running up and down the stairs, and then finally, I ran into the neighbor's house. I was actually in his kitchen searching for sweets. I heard the neighbor say, "Who is there?" I remember he finished his shower quickly and came out of the bathroom, abruptly, in only a towel, to see who it was.

UNSHAKABLE

I didn't have time to run out because I was on the other side of the kitchen or I am pretty sure I would have scrammed from there — just for the fact that I was in his cabinets. He saw me and I said I wasn't doing anything and shrugged. He must have said something like, "Oh, it's just you," to make light of the situation. He then said, "Hold on," and went into the bathroom to quickly change. When he came out, he walked over to the living room and called me over from the kitchen. Innocently, I did as he asked.

He then told me he was going to do yoga and asked me if I wanted to try it. I said sure, not really knowing what yoga was. He then told me to lie on the floor on my back so he could show me a move. Carelessly, I said, "Okay." But then he got on all fours and moved on top of me in the opposite direction. He lowered his whole groin area over my face. I felt his private press against my face, and I thought, "That's it!"

"I GOT TO GO, DUDE, I GOT TO GO!" I shouted. He said, "No no no no no, shhhh, be quiet, it's just a game." I didn't care. I ran down the stairs and told my mom. She and my grandma confronted him, but he said I lied and said I was upstairs playing while he was in the shower.

My mom sort of threatened him and said, "You better not have done something like that."

But then that was it. He went back upstairs, and I was banned from ever going near him, which was fine. But in the end, I felt like I was the one to blame. I questioned myself ...What had I done? Why did I arouse him? Am I a disgusting little girl?

DISTANT MEMORIES

On another occasion, my art teacher pinned me against the school wall, pressed against me, and practically breathed into my mouth, literally an inch from my lips touching his. I said nothing. Why? Because I knew no one would believe or defend me. I just knew he was weird and stayed away from him.

Another time, I remember walking down the hallway and quickly glancing into his office. He was in there with the lights off, which seemed weird. When saw me, he said, "Come here, I will give you candy."

I thought, *Heck no, I know your kind all too well*. What I learned from these experiences in those critical years of life was this: *Every man was a pervert and a predator.*

Then there were my grandma's old friends from the bar who would sleep in our basement and try to touch my sisters and me. We got so used to it that we would go into battlefield mode — such rascals, right? "Okay Sis, you run down first. I will distract him while you quickly put the clothes in the wash, then on the count of three we run for our lives." It was so sad that after a while we made it a game to see who could get out quicker.

> I thought, *Heck no, I know your kind all too well.*

Rossie and her neighborhood friend

CHAPTER 2

Roots

What I did know was that the little girl inside me knew I was meant to be someone great. I remember when I was about eight years old, I would sing in front of an abandoned fence post and pretend I was a famous singer, then chant "...because I am Rossie — with sass." I remember that little girl quite clearly. I was always full of life.

People said that I was the kind of kid who would change the atmosphere as soon as I walked into a room. My confidence and smile are what changed the hearts around me. I was life-giving, caring, and happy. But, after the calamity I experienced, there were times in my life when I found myself in deep holes. I was alone and climbing out, only to fall back in again. When I finally called for help, real help, a supernatural Helper perfectly orchestrated my escape to a life of freedom — freedom from the darkness.

Unfortunately, we learned from a young age that we couldn't trust anyone, not even a father figure, because he hurt us, too. Our dad did not physically harm us, rather he hurt us emotionally through his rejection of us. We always wondered why his street life mattered more to him than we did. My sister reminded me of something recently. She said, "Do you remember when we used to stare out the kitchen window just watching on Saturday mornings to see if we saw Dad's 1990 Grand Marquis driving down the alley? Or when we heard a car drive down the alley, we would rush to the window with our angelic eyes and chant, 'It's Dad, it's Dad,' only to be disappointed because it wasn't?

UNSHAKABLE

I do remember spending a lot of time just staring out the window and imagining that our superhero was going to arrive and sweep his three little girls off their feet. In my mind, he would wrap his arms around us and just love us unconditionally. Our hearts were aching for unconditional love and affection, by two parents under one home, but we didn't get it. Our parents didn't know how to show unconditional love or even how to simply say, "I love you." I don't blame my mom, because I know she did her best and was coping with her own traumas. She was fatherless and motherless at the age of four when grandma went to prison for ten years, and my grandpa took off for good never to be seen or heard from again.

As my mom tells it, she can remember the day when the police came banging on the door looking for her mother. The next thing she can recall is seeing her mom handcuffed in a courtroom and being sentenced to ten years in prison. She can remember that as her mother was taken away, she asked a family member to give her a pear that was in the courtroom. To this day, she loves pears.

Then she was gone, leaving her seven children behind. By the time her mom (my grandmother) got out, my mother was almost 15 years old and hated my grandmother. She was the youngest and saw the family burdened with the responsibility to step in as a caregiver. My Aunt Ruby, who was 18 and the eldest, took the younger of the four plus my baby niece, and the others went their own way. My mother saw firsthand the effects of neglect and abandonment, and the destruction it brought to her brothers and sisters. Unfortunately, we lost two, one from cirrhosis of the liver and the other from AIDS.

ROOTS

This is only a snapshot of the unfortunate events that occurred in my family's lineage, but it goes beyond that. It is rooted in Mexico and the impoverished barrio in the city of Irapuato, Guanajuato.

Even now, there is a lot of healing that needs to be done in my family. I continue to pray, stand in the gap to break every chain and bondage in my lineage, and trust God to heal every broken wound. And one day He will, for He has overcome the world!

My dad was one of nine and mostly the family reject. I don't know much of my dad's story, but I know he was born and raised in Mexico in the small town of Tarrengito, Jalisco. I have been told that my dad's mom was disappointed in him for being an alcoholic. His brothers said my dad started to drink at a young age and that it took over his life.

Growing up, it seemed as if all of this was normal. Most kids in our area were in a similar unhealthy cycle, if not worse, so it was nothing new under the sun. Life continued.

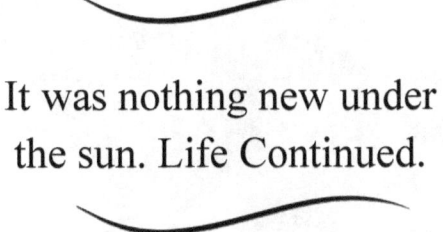

> It was nothing new under the sun. Life Continued.

Papa, Nancy and me

Ruby (left), Ruthy, Mom,
Peter, Christina, & Baby Priscilla

Mom & Us

Mom, Marilyn, Sophia, Nancy, and me

God is your answer!

CHAPTER 3

My Career Journey Begins

In the spring of 2012, at the age of 22, I began my career as an intern draftswoman working for a metal company. This wasn't my ideal position, but it was the only offer on the table at that time. Just getting this offer took a year of countless attempts to land a job in civil engineering.

I graduated from MATC with an associate degree in Civil Engineering Technology in 2011. After graduation, I submitted resumes and heard nothing. I took my search a step further and personally walked into engineering firms to deliver my resume only to be turned away. I didn't know why no one would hire me. Was it because I was straight out of a community college with no experience? Was it because I was a woman, not to mention a Latina, with no prior experience in a male-dominated trade? Ten years ago, it was rare to see women in engineering roles, and if so, they were university-level students.

The frustration was real as I took jobs at local coffee shops and tutored on the side. I was a kid from the ghetto who had attended a community college. I also carried around excessive baggage from my childhood and adolescent years. I thought about the things I didn't get and that life was so unfair. Self-pity became a roadblock and a barrier to moving forward. It was always about where I didn't go and who I wasn't. I was mostly offended by everyone. I was hurt and I blamed others for my self-rejection.

UNSHAKABLE

My mindset continually repeated, *Why was I not smart enough? Why couldn't my mother put me in a university? Why was my dad an alcoholic and why did he abandon us? What is wrong with me? Why wasn't I loved? Why do I get hurt every time I open my heart to someone? And now, in the professional world, it's all the same. It's unfair, life is unfair.*

Joyce Meyer says it this way, "Self-pity leaves us feeling hopeless, and that is one of the worst feelings in the world. It leads to depression and prevents us entirely from seeing good things that we do have." Then she goes on, saying, "You can be pitiful or powerful, but you can't be both."

For me, self-pity was a battlefield of the mind and I hated myself as a result of it. I was beautiful on the outside, but on the inside, I was ugly and falling apart. I had deeply rooted wounds covered by bandages that were oozing and seeping whenever an emotional event occurred or when something triggered my past. The constant rejection was relentless.

Did you know that the brain doesn't know time? If a past event is triggered by something in the present, then your brain brings back all the associated emotions as if it just happened and we tend to act on those emotions. So if a negative emotion is triggered, it may result in a coping skill like anger or we might make irrational decisions. Until we learn to retrain our brains, and maybe even give those emotions to God, our patterns of behavior will not change.

Ultimately, my job search revealed that I didn't know how to live a life of freedom, joy, and peace when things weren't going my way. To be fair, it is rare that young people do. But, I put myself in bondage and made irrational and desperate decisions time and time again during this period that nearly cost me my life.

Believe me when I tell you that you can heal from your past. The shame and guilt are no longer yours. You can set the past at Jesus' feet, and He will take it from you. I wish I had known then what I know now, and I desperately want to share this with you. You must be willing to let go of your shame and guilt because He won't do it for you. You have to be willing and you have to want it.

You have to *want* to live a life of freedom. Living life every day in freedom is a choice you make across all areas of your life — at work, school, home, at the bus stop, and even at church. Yes, even at church, because Christians are not perfect either. We will never be perfect, there is only one perfect person and that's God Himself — the creator of this world.

"You can be pitiful or powerful, but you can't be both."

UNSHAKABLE

You can take that first step toward a life of freedom today by saying, "I want to be set free." You can make the choice to be set free from negative emotions, hurt, pain, immorality, stress, and anxiety, free from anything that steals your joy and peace. You can choose to be saved and to live in the perfect peace that transcends all understanding in your life. For we are told, *But he was pierced for our transgressions; he was crushed for our iniquities (sin); upon him was the chastisement (correction) that brought us peace, and with his wounds we are healed.* (Matthew 20:5)

A technique that I find very beneficial is from the **Praying Medic – Emotional Healing in 3 Easy Steps.**

In short, you identify an emotion that you associate with an event, ask for the emotion to be taken from you, and then ask that your soul be healed. The key is to get to the familiar place where those emotions are triggered, and we do this by storytelling with a trusted friend or spiritual advisor. When we get to that place of trauma, where the tears become so heavy and when the heart aches, then it is time to stop and recognize the hurt. Promptly pray over the situation, ask for forgiveness for yourself or any sinful behavior, and give it to the Lord. Ask Him to heal the broken wound, take the emotions away from you, and replace them with something good.

I witnessed my friend become set free by doing this. It was a three-hour process, but well worth the wait! We had to dig deep, 20-30 years deep, and it was life-changing. We felt a shift in the atmosphere; we felt the bondage break off and her heart mended and healed by God.

Now, that's victory! For He says, *Cast all your cares on him, for he cares for you.* (1 Peter 5:7)

"Mountain High Rossie"

God is your answer!

CHAPTER 4

Resilience

What I didn't recognize in my career journey to that point, was that I truly AM an overcomer. I am uncommon. I am smart and educated. And, I almost believed the lie of the enemy! But, I am resilient and I persevered. I did not allow the enemy to keep me from completing my coursework despite the challenges I faced.

I graduated from college in 2011, as one of two women in my class of what society calls a "man's trade". I was a mom who had just escaped an abusive relationship and was raising a one-year-old boy. Seriously, thank God for MATC's onsite daycare. I remember dropping *"Mr. Sunshine"* off at daycare in the mornings before class. I was able to visit him between classes and breastfeed him! Then, after an eight-hour day, off we went back home to our little one-bedroom apartment.

How many times do we get so wrapped up in our circumstances that we let doubt have its way? We don't move forward, we end up growing weary and stagnant. Think for a minute. What is something that you have accomplished, big or small? It could be from childhood, a science project, getting your high school diploma or GED, or making your first home-cooked meal, anything that made you feel proud of yourself. Next time doubt sets in, think of those things because you have the drive and the mind of Christ. You have what it takes to accomplish your heart's desire. Don't give up, keep moving and keep on knocking on doors of opportunity. Let every 'no' push you even harder to achieve your goal.

That is what I did, and after some time, I was finally offered a position as a draftswoman almost a full year after graduating. This is where I learned to serve, and I did it well.

UNSHAKABLE

I didn't question why I got the hand-me-down work, or why I folded hundreds of D-sized plan sheets, continually paper-cutting my fingers. I was just happy that I finally had a job and was in an organization full of engineers and professionals. It made me feel important.

I thought to myself, *This must be it; this must be my ticket to success, this must be my entry-level position to get in, to feel elite*. Doesn't every kid who was raised by a single mother and an alcoholic father in the ghetto feel that way? Doesn't every rebellious runaway teen who found acceptance from local gangs and who was once date raped feel that way? I did! I had finally turned my life around, became someone important, and changed my narrative in life. I made it!

> This must be it; this must be my ticket to success, this must be my entry-level position to get in, to feel elite.

What I failed to realize in that moment was all of those things were what made me resilient. The failures had become my ticket to success. They were my preparation for becoming a warrior! What the enemy meant for evil, my God turned around and used for His good.

For I know the plans I have for you declares the Lord, plans to prosper you and not to harm you, plans to give you hope and a future. (Jeremiah 29:11)

"Mr. Sunshine" Anthony and me

God is your answer!

CHAPTER 5

Identity

This all sounds nice, right? I finally landed a job, moved on from my past, and lived happily ever after with my son. So why don't we end it here, you ask? Because that is not the end of my story, and ending it here would be a lie.

After some time in that entry-level position, I was finally hired as a full-time employee with a one-dollar-per-hour increase to my hourly wage. I thought life was good, even though I was living from paycheck to paycheck and sometimes had to make ends meet with only $20 left to my name after I paid my bills and bought groceries. My son and I lived simply. I was content.

You may be asking where my baby daddy was. He was around. But he, like me, was young and naïve. We were living la vida loca, the crazy life. At that time, my heart was chasing after experiences and doing whatever I could to win approval from those around me when I was at home. When I was at work, I was trying to hide my shameful past, code-switching between the real me and the classy professional that I wanted the world to view me as.

There is nothing wrong with chasing after experiences or being classy and professional. But I was doing so while desperately trying to hide my true character and appeal to others. At home, I lived la vida loca and at work I presented myself as a professional, meaning I was not being my authentic self at either place. In the best of circumstances, this is difficult.

UNSHAKABLE

We Latinas have a certain spice, color, and boldness to us. So, why did I try to hide that from my co-workers? Well, it's quite simple, I was afraid I would be rejected at work for breaking the conventional view of the typical Latina.

I was a credential-holic! I was man-pleasing! Of course, I was! My dad abandoned us. I had no other father figure in my life. The men I did have in my life only abused me both physically and mentally. I was trying to fix my trauma and find my identity in the professional world.

I was to learn that you can't move on if you've got junk in the trunk.

> I was to learn that you can't move on if you've got junk in the trunk.

God is your answer!

CHAPTER 6

Falling Through the Cracks

Fast forward to six months after my permanent hire. A new manager joined the company and began to review policies, job duties, and compensation. One morning, he called me into his office and told me to sit down. *Oh no, what did I do wrong?* I wondered. At 22 years old, I was in sheer terror of my new boss and had not yet built the self-confidence to meet with him.

When I entered the room, he asked me how I liked the company and thanked me for my service. Meanwhile, my mind was racing, *This is it. He is letting me go, I'm going to get fired.*

John Bevere says:

"People who have been rejected by a father or leader, tend to take all the blame on themselves. They are imprisoned by tormenting thoughts of 'What did I do?' and 'Was my heart impure?' Then constantly try to prove their innocence to their leaders. They think that if they can only show their loyalty and value, they will be accepted. Sadly, the more they try, the more rejected they feel."

This describes exactly how I lived, with tormenting thoughts, blaming myself, and doing whatever I could to please "man." And, now I sat before my new boss and heard him explain that after reviewing my job duties and compensation, he realized that I was only making $12 per hour. He then told me that he saw my potential and felt that I could move up in the organization quickly. He ended the conversation by saying that I would be receiving an increase in my wages to $13 per hour. I was inspired. I was happy. I was finally seeing hard work pay off.

UNSHAKABLE

Unfortunately, that feeling would not last and I would fall through the cracks between my profession and personal life at home. Just a short time after meeting with my boss, I went on a three-day drinking and cocaine binge and ended up losing my job. My behavior exposed something deeply rooted within me. I still had an "I don't give a S*** attitude." I thought I was the one in control of my life. I felt stuck. I felt trapped. I felt alone. So, I caved in. I gave up. It felt as though the world had devoured me.

On a personal level, I was a single mother just getting by. I drove a loud trap car, struggled to pay the bills, and moved from place to place. I had to give up the one-bedroom apartment where my son and I lived. I just couldn't afford it anymore and it brought back memories, both good and bad, of my son's father.

At about this same time, Wisconsin had passed a new law requiring car insurance. It was just my luck that every time I drove through the industrial park on my way to work, my loud muffler gained attention. I was pulled over numerous times. I received so many tickets that I don't even remember why anymore. But at least two were because I did not have auto insurance. When I lost my license as a result of the tickets, I felt like the world was against me. Like, come on! How can a single mother, just getting by, fresh out of school in an attempt to rewrite her story, receive no compassion or empathy? I fell back into my old mindset. *I'm just not lucky. I'm not good enough. I am especially not worthy.*

Looking back, I should have slapped myself and said, "Snap out of it! It's just the base of the rollercoaster. There's nowhere to go but up!"

"There's nowhere to go but up!"

God is your answer!

CHAPTER 7
The Last Straw

I would have been wrong though. The last straw came when I learned I was facing a felony charge. I had gotten into a fight with a girl at the Sturtevant Cinco De Mayo Rodeo about a month prior to losing my job. It was supposed to be a Sunday funday with the girls. We were dressed up all cute and carpooled to the event. We were super excited to dance and maybe find a cute cowboy.

While I was dancing, I saw a fight break out in the distance near the bar area. People began running and stepping over one another as bottles flew through the air. It was radical and crazy, it actually reminded me of a stampede. I started to look for my girls and found two, but could not see Tracy. They told me that she was in the fight as we ran to the scene. When we arrived, I saw a man grab Tracy from behind and I remember thinking, *That's it, he better get off of her*, and I flung an empty beer bottle at him.

Then, unfortunately for me, a 15-year-old jumped on me from the back and we began to fight and roll on the floor. Even though she jumped me, ultimately the law was in her favor, because she was a minor.

Plus, her daddy had money which meant power and revenge. And NOW he was taking me to court for child abuse — a felony! I was thinking, *Come on, seriously. A petty girl fight?* I had done so many terrible things in my teen years, including gang activity and selling drugs. Could it be that time was catching up with me and this was my punishment?

> And NOW he was taking me to court for child abuse — a felony!

As I sat in the county jail for three days not knowing if I was going to be set free, all I could think about was my two-year-old son and my now messed-up future. Luckily, my friends bailed me out and I was able to go back to work. But, I had to go through the process of trying to find a lawyer and repaying my bail, not to mention dealing with the rumors from family and friends.

I was a wreck! I had no money! I had an ugly car and no willpower! I was an embarrassment at work and to my family! And, of course, I had the worst mugshot ever!

God is your answer!

CHAPTER 8

Caving In

You would have thought that would have straightened me out, but it didn't. I gave up and caved in. I went on a drinking binge and began to live in darkness again, the darkness from my teen and early adolescent years before my son was born. My soul was weak, I was weak. I was the seed that was tossed on the path that the birds quickly came to eat and devour, instead of the seed that was planted in good soil and produced good fruit, representing someone who maintains their integrity even through difficult times and clings to Jesus and His word.

From the gospel of Matthew:

When anyone hears the message about the kingdom and does not understand it, the evil one comes and snatches away what was sown in their heart. This is the seed sown along the path. The seed falling on rocky ground refers to someone who hears the word and at once receives it with joy. But since they have no root, they last only a short time. When trouble or persecution comes because of the word, they quickly fall away. The seed falling among the thorns refers to someone who hears the word, but the worries of this life and the deceitfulness of wealth choke the word, making it unfruitful. But the seed falling on good soil refers to someone who hears the word and understands it. This is the one who produces a crop, yielding a hundred, sixty or thirty times what was sown. (Matthew 13:19-23)

UNSHAKABLE

Thanks to my Auntie Chris, I was saved as a child and I knew about God and His Word. You see when we were little, Auntie Chris lived with us in our three-bedroom duplex that housed my mom, grandmother, and three of us kids.

She was on track to getting her life right with the Lord and up until I was in middle school, Auntie Chris and her dear friend, Uncle Roy (R.I.H.), would take me to church on Sundays. Auntie worked long hours, but nevertheless, planted seeds in our hearts, reminding us that God's word and love would never depart from us. I knew my salvation was secured, even if I stepped into the darkness. But this knowledge gave me a false sense of security and it was dangerous.

> Auntie Chris …
> planted seeds in our hearts,
> reminding us that
> God's word and love would
> never depart from us.

I tried God's patience on many occasions. I played with fire and ooooh, did I get burned. When I fell through the cracks, relying on myself instead of God, I'm certain I tried His patience. But, His patience should not be confused with tolerance. Rather, this was a time when God was waiting for me while I was lost in the world.

God is your answer!

CHAPTER 9
The Pit

And so, after a year of heavy drinking, cocaine, and partying, I found myself in a pit. Running the streets from place to place wasn't doing me any favors; it doesn't for anyone. To this day, I thank Jesus that I didn't become addicted to crack or heroin, or that I wasn't trafficked for that matter. I was once given crack at the age of 12. I had gone to a crack house with a family member one day and saw for myself what it looked like. I saw those poor lost souls screaming to be set free from their abyss of addiction, and it frightened me. I knew I never wanted to be like that, but the path I was headed on went in the same direction.

When I finally snapped out of it, I was in a pit of hopelessness. I couldn't go any deeper. I was at rock bottom by the age of just 24, and was in the process of being evicted from our home. I knew something needed to change and that I needed to wake up.

My only excuse is that it's hard when all you know is party and booze. The party life was all too familiar because that is what was all around me as I grew up. I did not know that a life outside of that was even possible for me. I thought violence was okay, fists of anger were acceptable, being vulgar was appropriate, disrespect meant power, and so on.

It took a long time for me to break the cycle and stop falling back into the familiar patterns of my life. It was like a love-hate relationship. Although I hated who I was becoming, I still loved it all the same. But each time I relapsed into my old ways, God saved me. He opened doors for me time and time again. I'm sure he thought, *You'll get it right someday, Honey.*

UNSHAKABLE

If I could share some knowledge today, I would urge anyone facing the same relapse scenarios in their life to understand that there is more to life than their past and that they can make a decision today to change their path if they truly let God guide them. It isn't going to be easy. I'm not going to lie. It's going to be the hardest thing they could ever do. That's why most people don't come out of the darkness and into the light. Look at National Avenue in Milwaukee. It breaks my heart watching the women sell themselves. I cry out for them because I know how worthless they feel. But they are not. They are beauty and splendor. They are a gift from God who knows their story. They were oppressed and taken advantage of; they were preyed on. Yes, everything is a choice, but some people don't ever see the light. All they know is chaos and calamity from birth. It's our responsibility to do something — even if it's prayer.

Defend the poor and fatherless; Do justice to the afflicted and needy. Deliver the poor and needy; Free them from the hand of the wicked. They do not know, nor do they understand; They walk about in darkness. (Psalm 82:3-5 NKJV)

After I hit rock bottom, I knew there needed to be a dramatic shift in my life. So, I mustered up my faith, the little that I had, and prayed. I am sure it was basic, something like *Please God, please help me, I promise I will be good.* But hey, that mustard seed of faith can move mountains!

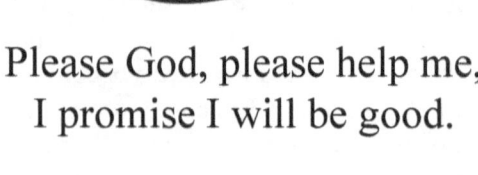

Please God, please help me,
I promise I will be good.

THE PIT

For truly I tell you, if you have faith the size of a mustard seed, you will say to this mountain, 'Move from here to there,' and it will move; and nothing will be impossible for you. (Matthew 17:20-21)

I may not have been living right, but I was saved! I knew God's Word and knew that it never comes back void, without having any effect. I had a little bit of light inside of me. It was faint and maybe almost out, but it was there. And I used it because my God is faithful and merciful and helps the brokenhearted, the oppressed, the fatherless, and the widow.

And that's what happened with the little bit of fire left in me. I managed to find care for my son at a local preschool. Then, a week later I got hired by a temp agency making $15 an hour as a computer-aided drafter. I was excited, I was blessed, I was back on track, and had hope once again.

Although my living situation was not ideal, at least I had a safe place to lay my head at night. I was living in an upstairs rooming house with a shared bathroom on top of a dear family friend's bar. He will always have a very special place in my heart; Don Blass — Te Quiero.

Up until I got the job at the temp agency, I had been bartending at night. Which meant late nights and working on the weekends. Starting this new job now enabled me to afford a place of my own and allowed me to quit bartending. Needless to say, I was very emotional and joyous.

God is your answer!

CHAPTER 10

Starting Fresh

I remember my first day at the New Berlin office where I had been hired by the temp agency. The people were kind and helped me get set up. The division I was in mostly worked on telecommunication design, coax, and fiber cables, something I knew nothing about. Still, I decided to pursue it and challenge myself. I thought to myself, *I can figure it out. I didn't come this far to fail again!*

I am not going to lie, the first couple of weeks I got by, but I remember thinking, What am I doing? I don't know what I am doing, why am I here? I began to doubt myself again. I fought between asking a potential 'stupid question' or not asking at all. In my mind, I thought, *I've got to get this right. I can't let my guard down, especially as a woman, right? That would give us a bad name in this trade*. Finally, I thought *This is stupid, I am going to go ask.*

Lucky for me, the lead person was very detail-oriented and a good teacher. He invited me into his office and showed me exactly how things were done. He explained municipality codes, permits, restrictions, and how to accurately read blueprints. I felt such a burden lift off of me. After that, I realized that I was in a unique place, and I asked as many questions as I could.

I quickly learned the telecommunications world because I didn't give up. How many of us want to throw in the towel the first couple of days, weeks, or months when faced with a challenge? Challenges are good. They build us up and if you want true success, it won't come without struggle. Failure isn't really a failure, it is a learning experience. Seek counsel and get help. It's okay to ask.

UNSHAKABLE

During my tenure, I was starting to become confident in my trade and it felt good. It was a feeling of self-assurance in my own qualities and abilities. I stayed the course, didn't give up, and laid a firm foundation for future success.

It wasn't easy, but I am glad I went through that period in life. I learned how to work hard, meet deadlines, write emails, and interact with others while making eye contact. I learned through trying, failing, and doing it again and again until I got it right. I wasn't afraid to make mistakes; they are the best part of learning. Remember 3rd grade and learning about the scientific method? Create a hypothesis and then test the theory. If the hypothesis is wrong, then do it again!

I also learned by asking questions. How many times are we afraid to ask questions, fearful that we might be looked down upon? As Craig Groeschel says, "It's not weakness to get help, it's wisdom." When you know your job and take the time to understand its intricacies, you foster trust and instill confidence. You gain experience and knowledge, and then you are able to build the staircase until you reach the next platform. We are always learning and always moving from place to place. Keep building and have an open mindset to try new things and challenge yourself. You never know what you can achieve until you try.

Our staff was growing which resulted in our move to the Butler location. We now had a private building with our own garage and owned company vehicles. During this time, I began to do outside plant design work and drove a company vehicle.

What I enjoyed the most were the long drives to Kenosha or Racine. It was a nice time to relax, listen to music, and of course, spend less time in the office. Furthermore, I was able to take a company vehicle home from time to time.

On one occasion, my car broke down. I had little money saved up and could not afford the rental fees. Nervously, I told my boss that I was not sure what to do. He happily told me to take one of the company cars home. Man, that was nice. He didn't have to do that, but he did. I will always appreciate Todd for helping me in those times of trouble and for hiring me even though I have a record. This job really did help me to move in the right direction. I thank God for that.

> "It's not weakness to get help, it's wisdom."

God is your answer!

CHAPTER 11
Rage and Rebellion

Meanwhile, life at home was chaotic. Remember when I said God pulled me out of my pit after a year of drugs and alcohol? Well, he pulled someone else out, too. Mario. He is now my husband, but in the past, he had been an accomplice to my miserable state of living.

Neither of us had fully given up all the junk of the world. We both lacked self-control. We worked during the week but would still drink on the weekends. When we had too much, we ended up fighting with one another, physically and emotionally.

We had so much rage from our pasts that we ended up taking it out on one another. On a few occasions, it got bad. I would grab objects and throw them at him. He, in turn, would strangle me. That's how we lived.

One time, when I was pregnant (and totally sober), I clawed his face because he wouldn't let me out of the room. The police said that wasn't reason enough for me to attack him and that I should be going to jail. It was only because of his mercy and the fact that I was seven months pregnant that they didn't take me out in handcuffs. Instead, I had to leave the house for the night and go upstairs to my mother's. I remember feeling disgusted and so much hate for him. I tried reasoning with the police officers that it was my house and that he was the one who needed to leave. This didn't happen, and instead, I went upstairs for the night, returning the next morning as if nothing happened. In the end, we were both one foot in and one foot out, which is very dangerous.

UNSHAKABLE

It reminds me of God's words, *You are either hot or cold, but not lukewarm or I will spit you out!* (Revelation 3:15-16) Yes, He said that, and He was sure right.

By the winter after my son was born, the physical and mental abuse became so regular that I decided to kick Mario out after another encounter. In addition to our son, my six-year-old from a previous relationship was living with us. I was now fighting for my life and the safety of my children. And what mother doesn't protect her children?

While not an excuse, the violence was nothing new to us. It was rooted in our family histories. My husband grew up with an abusive father who beat his mother during alcoholic episodes. As a young boy, he watched until he grew strong enough to fight back for her. One day, at the age of 13, he picked up a bat and beat his father. Then he ran away from home and never returned.

My rage comes from people dear to me, those who spoke non-affirming words and used hateful speech towards me. And those pans, belts, and shoes only added to my rage. My sister reminded me of something critical, asking if I remembered writing hate letters in my diary. She added that looking back, she was sorry for what I had gone through. I must have been about 12 years old when I had that diary. Thankfully, I have forgiven the people that I wrote about so long ago. But, this is a good reminder that words have power, the power to crush someone, so choose yours wisely. Are you speaking words of life or death? Because life and death are in the power of the tongue. If you aren't careful, you have the ability to curse someone and cause so much harm. So speak life into every situation.

In addition to the rage in me, I had honed my fighting skills in battles during high school, on grocery store runs, and simply from all the hatred built up inside of me. I was a ganger and thought it was an honor to jump people.

RAGE AND REBELLION

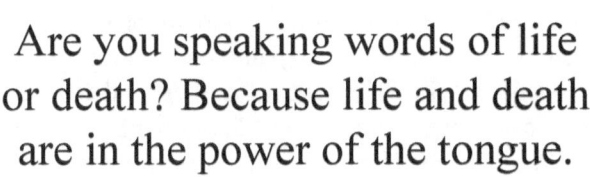

Are you speaking words of life or death? Because life and death are in the power of the tongue.

We once jumped a girl in an alley because she rolled with another gang. An ex-boyfriend of mine said it this way while staring at me with such compassionate eyes "What happened to my beautiful rose?" His words hurt me. Then he broke up with me. I was 16 at that time. At that moment, I laughed. But, now I look back and see exactly what he meant. Metaphorically, I had died. The thorns had taken over my life and the weeds had overtaken me. My light wasn't shining anymore.

I was a troubled, rebellious teen who thought I knew everything. Why was I so wicked, abusing someone for pleasure and gain, at 16? It came from the childhood hate, neglect, and abuse that had built up inside of me. I didn't deal with it well. I didn't know who to turn to. I was once a young girl so in love with Jesus, and now I walked a path of wickedness.

I turned and went backward; I ran in the opposite direction from Jesus. I was looking for love and acceptance at all costs, even at the expense of others, and even if that meant preying on others. In my mind, I was just paying society back. And those nights with rolled-up marijuana laced with cocaine, as I reminisced about the past, made it all the better.

UNSHAKABLE

When I was 16, I ran away with some girlfriends I met. We ended up staying at a local trap house with a bunch of gang members. An older friend had her license so we were able to hitch rides everywhere with her. I remember we drank bottles of E&J, got homemade tattoos, and smoked marijuana. Once, while we were all sitting in the car, another rival gang came with bats and bashed the windows and doors while we were sitting there smoking weed. They took off, while we were left to clean up all the glass that had fallen on us. The next day we cleaned the car, cut a fake door out of a cardboard box, and then rode through the south side swerving and looking for our rivals.

On another occasion, we got shot up by another gang on 16th Street and Cesar Chavez Drive. We were walking down 16th Street celebrating the festivities when we heard a bunch of bullets being fired at us and the guys. In an instant, one bullet hit my friend who was standing right next to me, and another bullet swiped right past my head, missing it only by a few inches. One of the guys also got hit. The next thing we knew, we heard sirens and saw the ambulances in the distance.

My life could have ended right there, at 16 with a silver bullet to my head. My family would have grieved and called me innocent while the news headline would say,

A HOMICIDE IN MILWAUKEE — RECKLESS TEENS AND GANG MEMBERS

And then, I would have woken up in hell. What a scary thought! But I didn't die. During the day, I would go home and sneak in through an open window to eat since everyone was off to school and work. If the window wasn't open, I would look for loose change on the sidewalks to buy myself a $1 chicken sandwich from McDonalds (during the good old dollar days).

RAGE AND REBELLION

Although I was a runaway, I was still very close to home, probably within a 10-block radius. Well, that life got boring and sad pretty quickly. My body couldn't take the drinking and the street fights anymore. I seriously would get a whiff of the E&J and want to vomit. To be cool I just pretended like I was drinking it. Then I would toss it out.

I started to miss home and school. One day, I thought it would be a good idea to stroll into school. I figured I could at least eat a good warm meal and see my sisters who I hadn't seen in weeks. So I did. I went to class. In an instant, security grabbed me and pulled me into the office. The man asked where I had been. I said, "I dunno." A cliche response from a teen, but clearly I did. They said they had to call the police and that my mom had been to the school in tears, crying for me and saying that I was missing.

I thought to myself, *Really, why would she do that? She hates me!* But she came and took me home. She grounded me for life and watched my every move. I couldn't stand it, so I eventually packed my bags and left again. I went to a cousin's house who allowed me to stay as long as I went to school. That was the caveat. Other than that, I continued to do whatever I wanted.

My cousin was a young mother and single, but older, and going through her own traumas. So we boozed it up, and when we couldn't pay rent, we sold drugs or borrowed electricity from the empty house next door with an extension cord through the window. My goodness, we were desperate! Then, at 18, I finally moved out, got a job, and forced myself through school.

God is your answer!

Rossie (age 16) and baby sis', Sophia

CHAPTER 12

Lucifer

Mario and I met in a bar, which meant our relationship had grown out of pleasure and party. I didn't know how to find love and value in myself. I thought my worth came out of giving myself up and being promiscuous. After I kicked Mario out, I met a man who was literally a Lucifer. He spoke lies and deceit and was very crafty. He promised me the world and I fell for it. Stupid me, when I was finally doing so well, I got sucked right back in. When I finally got out, when I finally wanted to get things right...I went backward again!

One time, a prophet from Texas spoke over me and said, "Girl, you need to stop taking one step forward and two steps backward." Man, that shocked me. I never had listened to prophets in the past, but I know I started to on that day because I understood exactly what he meant.

Lucifer showered me with dates and flowers, something that I had never experienced. He showed love and affection to my children to win me over. He called almost constantly to tell me how much he missed me and I believed his lies. He said he had a job and was in the music industry on the side. He talked about family and a life free from alcohol and drugs. He said all the things I wanted to hear.

STOP! Be wary of anyone who repeatedly reminds you of their love and constantly reaffirms you, especially right after meeting them. I fell for it. I was desperate for love and I thought, *This is it*. Maybe the signs were there or maybe I chose to turn the other cheek.

UNSHAKABLE

After a few months, things got serious and I let him move in with me. Little did I know, this would be one of the biggest mistakes of my life.

On one occasion, we got invited to a birthday party at a local bar and decided to go even though we didn't drink. When we got there, we saw familiar friends, some mutual and some not. After about half an hour or so he wanted to leave, which made me a little confused. When we walked out of the bar and were about halfway down the block, a friend came out and shouted, *"Hey sis!"* I turned and loudly replied, *"YES?"* She said, "Come here," but he grabbed my arm and said, *"Let's go!"*

I was torn. A part of me wanted to go and see what she had to say, but the other half of me wanted to ignore her and so I did. Little did I know, she was trying to save me from this man. She was trying to save my life because she knew he was up to no good. When we got to his house, he played the romantic role and said things every woman wants to hear. Then the time came and you know the rest. The next day I was brainwashed!

As the weeks went by things were good. But I started to notice a trend. He wasn't going to work. He also admitted that the car he drove wasn't his. It belonged to a friend of his who let him borrow her car. I found out later it was his sugar momma's car. I learned that he claimed disability and sold his pain pills to make a living. He was also on Section 8 which helped him pay for his nice apartment.

One day, his older daughter came over. I found out that she was addicted to heroin when he let her shoot up in the bathroom. I thought, *Are you serious?* Eventually, it got to the point where he would drop me off at work and then pick me up after because he had to give the car back to his sugar momma. (Pendeja!) I was disgusted. I was finding things out little by little that made me just want to curl up in a ball and cry.

LUCIFER

At last, I finally packed my bags and left my own house. I sent him a message telling him that he could stay at my house until he found a place. In the meantime, I went back to stay with my mom.

A week later, he moved out and I was able to go back home, finally relieved that this guy was gone. But was he really gone? I began to get text messages from him almost immediately. He said he was going to kill me. He started calling and calling non-stop. It sounded like he was on pills or something.

Now that I think about it, I don't know why I didn't call the police. Oh, that's right! He told me he left a bag of cocaine in the house and that I was going to go down for it! I had enough experience with that when I was charged with a felony, so the police were not on my agenda.

The person I called instead was Mario and he quickly came over. We packed up and went somewhere for the night, then decided to move into another home. We did this in only a month's time, and he promised that our new life would be better...after he blamed me for the mess I made. He said that the kids deserved better and that it was my fault for everything.

This is called manipulation! Keep in mind that I had lived with this shame and guilt for some time. According to *Manipulation: Signs and Behaviors in Relationships* (verywellmind.com), people who manipulate use mental distortion and emotional exploitation to influence and control others. Their intent is to have power and control over others to get what they want. They use tactics like gaslighting, passive-aggressive behavior, lying, blaming, threats, coerciveness, withdrawal, withholding, and isolation. They know your weakness and use it against you!

God is your answer!

CHAPTER 13

Perfect Love

Mario and I got back together after he rescued me from Lucifer. He helped me move out, we got married by the court and lived together as a family. I was desperate. Who could ever love me again the way I was? Was I branded and burnt for life?

This time, we only lasted six months before the abuse started up. Once again, I found myself alone and broken. I couldn't comprehend life anymore. Why, when I loved, couldn't I be loved back?

In all honesty, I didn't want to live. I felt lifeless and void. I kept it hidden deep inside and managed to keep my job. I knew I had children to support, so that meant that even if I was broken and hurting inside, I still needed to do what I had to do to keep food on the table and pay the rent.

To this day, the perfect love I searched for is not found. I know now that it can never be found in man, as this is an unconditional love; a love that never fails, and a love that knows you inside and out. It is a love that is kind and gentle, that knows your every need. It can mend and heal wounds, and is truthful, honest, and never lies. It is a love that is my protection, my strong tower. It is a love that whispers and a love I had never experienced until now.

That love is Jesus! He is a gentle and kind-spirited person; a friend, a husband, and a comforter who heard me in my time of need. He hears you in your time of distress, too. When you feel worthless and blotted out, He hears you. He hears you even when you feel like the scum of the earth. He counts every tear, even those almost tears.

> The only person who can help you recover from all of your trauma is Jesus.

The only person who can help you recover from all of your trauma is Jesus. He can truly take those unpleasant emotions away. This is the love that I had been in search of all my life.

I had another dream that may help you understand. I was walking down a road paved with smooth rocks. It was a nice day and I could see people all around. We were all heading toward the same place and all following along this path. I then looked over and saw a man. He was a gentle man with the most beautiful eyes ever. He gazed at me with such love, with a stare I had never seen before. In that moment, I felt that unconditional love that I had been in search of my whole entire life to this point.

He then held my hand and we continued to walk the path with the others. Once we got to our destination, we were home and at a place of rest. I laid down and he laid down next to me so we were side-by-side. Then he gazed at me with love one more time. I will never forget those eyes, because the love was all in his eyes when he looked at me. They were the softest, blue-green eyes I had ever seen.

He was a perfect man, pure and spotless. Then I slept and rested; all was well.

I truly believe that was Jesus in my dream; showing me the way, the easy road, if I would just give Him my hand and follow. He was showing me His perfect gentle love. I know it was Jesus in this dream.

Anthony and Nico

God's Love and His Creation

God is your answer!

CHAPTER 14

Transition

After the fourth year of working for the same company, I had reached the end of my growth journey. I wasn't moving up and I hoped to do more. I excelled at everything I did because part of who I am is a very driven gal. I have an '*I will figure it out and excel at it*' kind of attitude. In a world full of pessimists, I am the optimist.

Around this time, I got into a disagreement with another employee about a design. He didn't like where I was going with the project and did not want to rework the design. Angrily, he shouted and insulted me in the workplace. I felt embarrassed. I was humiliated and belittled. But, because he was a middle-aged, white man, I froze and didn't have the courage to say a thing. I walked away to my desk and just sat there in emptiness. Then I went to the bathroom, and in the stall, tears began to fall from my eyes. I'm telling you, that bathroom had seen a lot of tears shed – especially from the chaos in my personal life. That was where I could cry and talk to God. The best part was, He heard ME! My Poppa always has and continues to hear me to this day.

Yes, I cried; I let it out. It's okay to let it out, don't ever let anyone tell you differently. The resilient part of me, adaptable and able to bounce back, wiped away the tears, looked in the mirror, and said, "I got this." I put my big girl pants on and walked out of there with my head held high.

The day after this incident, I felt compelled to tell the manager. He listened with empathy and said he would speak to the person. The next day the manager called me into his office and told me that I was the one in the wrong and that it would be best if the other employee and I did not communicate with each other.

UNSHAKABLE

Can you believe that? I was in shock. I was dumbfounded! This isn't how you run an organization. We have to fix the problem, not avoid it. Clearly, yelling at someone in rage is not acceptable behavior!

Again, I said nothing. I stayed silent. I didn't react. I did not retaliate. I did not pick up worldly weapons. I was oppressed, but even in the oppression, I stayed faithful. I persevered under pressure and held my temper.

And guess what my God did? He opened the doors for employment at a government agency. I would be making more than one-and-a-half times my salary. I had a felony on my name from when I was 23, and they still hired me!

I was blessed! I was heard! He counted every tear, and said "Honey, the time is NOW, let's go, pack up your bags."

After giving two week's notice, of course. Then I walked out of there like a true child of God with a crown on my head! By the way, people say that they admire my child-like faith. Well, that's what it's all about. God wants you to have true faith even when everything seems to be falling apart.

And the Lord went before them by day in a pillar of cloud to lead the way, and by night a pillar of fire to give them light, so as to go by day and by night. He did not take away the pillar of cloud by day or the pillar of fire by night from before the people. (Exodus 13:21-22)

TRANSITION

God led me by a pillar of fire by night and a pillar of cloud by day. He was a light unto my feet. It might have been a dim light at times, but it was a light that never went out. I took baby steps, but those baby steps triumphed. When it was time to move, He told me to move, and I moved! He has never ceased taking me from place to place and He never will. I love it. I am to the point where I am like, *What's next God?*

God is your answer!

CHAPTER 15

Finding the Light

My life at home was still chaotic. My home was in ruins, the foundation was shaken, and the walls collapsed metaphorically and spiritually. My life was in shambles, and my soul was in despair. My spirit was lifeless, and my body was in agony and I knew this. I believe this is why I mustered up enough strength to make it to church one day.

I went during the season of Passover. You gotta love God's timing! It must have been late March or early April. On that day I cried, and I cried a lot. I was a 27-year-old woman who had finally given up but went to the right place this time. I went back into His loving hands, in unity with His people. I was so broken inside. My heart ached for change and it ached for healing from a heart so bitter, angry, and hurt.

I remember walking into the church and being greeted by some really nice people. Then I went into the sanctuary and found a seat in the back row. It was dark and looked very theatrical with lots of bright lights illuminating the altar and spotlighting the singers. Music began to play, and I just felt the comfort of the melodies. I began to let go of all the tension, the stress, and pride. I let myself become vulnerable and luckily for me, it was dark inside so that I could pour out my soul.

When the next song came on, the words just hit all the tender spots within me. I felt tears roll down my cheeks and then began to sob. I asked God to forgive me and to love me. I asked Him to take all my hopelessness away. I asked Him to take the guilt and shame off of me and told Him I was so sorry for being a wretch. I can't even tell you what song that was, but I believe it was sung for me that day.

UNSHAKABLE

God knew the day and hour when I needed Him the most. And he knows I love music, which can set the soul free. King David knew that, too. The Book of Psalms, nearly half of which were written by King David, are sacred songs and poems that are meant to be sung. King David, who went through many of the same battles we go through today, wrote his psalms to commemorate his life's events. His story is a powerful one, and I encourage you to read it when you have time.

Even today, when I find myself in despair, I open Psalms and read David's hymns and praises. They are life unto my lips, food to my belly, and have the power to change my soul. For he says, *Why are you downcast, oh my soul? Why so disturbed within me? Put your hope in God, for I will yet praise him. My savior and my God.* (Psalms 42:5)

My soul was downcast and I was running from the enemy. I was tormented by the enemy. All I could think about was the bad, the negative, and the ugly. My soul was disturbed. I was not at peace and I was condemning myself over and over again when God had already paid the price for my salvation by forgiving my sins.

> I said in a whisper, "Lord, I can't fix myself, You have to."

FINDING THE LIGHT

I truly believe this is why people don't come to the Father. They condemn themselves and feel like they are not good enough or righteous enough. Instead of clinging to the Father, they run farther away. I say this because I did that many times. I would say things like, "Well, I already screwed up, and I am too shameful to be accepted by any church or God, so cheers to another." This is wrong thinking, and quite frankly, a lot of churches in the United States make people feel this way, far too often. Well, Faith Builders did not and I love them tenderly for that.

That day in church, when all was said and done, I said in a whisper, "Lord, I can't fix myself, You have to." I could not fix myself and neither can you. He has to do all the work within us. But will we trust Him even in the midst of the storms? I did. My foundation had to be broken, so He could rebuild me because the Father dwells in each of His believers, not in the church building. When we come together, we make up the church as members of one body. Therefore, we must ensure that the temple of our body is clean and open to accept Him and we do that by accepting the Lord Jesus Christ as our personal savior. He can wash us clean from all our sins with His precious blood.

If we confess our sins, he is faithful and just and will forgive us our sins and purify us from all unrighteousness. (1 John 1:9)

God is your answer!

Hope through finding the Light

CHAPTER 16

True Growth

Little did I know, this was the beginning of my true growth journey and the next stage in my life that opened the doors to pursue my purpose and destiny. It was also the beginning of spiritual warfare. The enemy DID NOT want me free. It was fine when I was riding along in darkness and falling into sin. But when I decided to make the true change for a personal relationship with God, the enemy attacked me, and I mean badly.

I remember being visited by demons while I was sleeping. I was mocked spiritually in my dreams by nasty demons I do not want to remember. I will tell you about one instance in particular, though. I was asleep in bed and during the middle of the night, I awakened. I had my eyes closed but felt a presence near me hovering over the bed. I opened my eyes and saw nothing. But my spirit saw him.

It may sound strange to an unbeliever who has never experienced this, but for me it was real. I saw the black silhouette of a man, very big, muscular, and strong. He was lustful and sweaty, and just stood there staring at me. I felt gross and scared. I pulled the covers over my head and began to pray. I prayed, "Dear Lord Jesus help me, please Jesus help me." Then it vanished and was gone. This was just one of many instances. I used to be attacked at least two to three times a month. My faith was weak and I knew little of the authority I had. So many times, I pleaded for Jesus to help me.

This happened even as a little girl. I can remember waking up many times and being strangled by my blanket. No one knew why, it just happened. The blankets would be twisted like a rope around my neck.

When I woke up, I would quickly loosen them, but the sound of me gasping for air would awaken the entire house. One night after an incident, my aunt took me into the bathroom and prayed over me. She told me to let it out, to go ahead and throw up.

As I said, the enemy wanted me even as an innocent child, even at birth, and he wants me again now since I have turned back to the Father. But I have learned how to defend myself during his spiritual attacks. I tell Satan and his little cockroaches to flee, that I am a child of God, and he can't touch me.

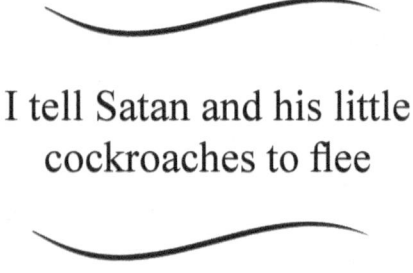

I tell Satan and his little cockroaches to flee

One time Jesus told me in a dream, very sternly, "So, rebuke the devil." He said it so clearly and simply, and I thought, *Oh yes, yes okay. I got it.* Because we are saved, we don't have to be afraid. We have the power and authority in us, which comes from the Holy Spirit when we accept Jesus Christ as our Lord and Savior. It took some time to understand this, but I am finally at a place where I have mastered it.

I am not sure what you are going through today, or if you are hurting deeply. But, what the enemy meant for evil in my life, God turned around and used for my good.

THE GROWTH

In some of my darkest moments, I did not hesitate to cry out to my heavenly Father. There are so many times when He used my pain to teach me to rely on His love and mercy.

One night, I remember being awakened by excruciating pain; my delicate flesh wounded and oozing. The burning, throbbing pain I experienced was debilitating as my skin infection grew worse and woke me up in the middle of the night. I cried as if I was in labor, feeling my flesh rip from my skin. *"Father!"* I yelled. Immediately I felt His soothing comfort heal my open wounds and I fell right back to sleep. That's grace; His grace. He is my Healer. He helped me endure the pain and find comfort in Him.

The man with leprosy on Jesus' way to Capernaum was my story. I sobbed the first time I saw the depiction in Joseph Prince's *Healing of the Leper* on YouTube. It depicts exactly how I felt and how I lived. I was an outcast, a miserable soul in a state of desperation. I didn't think anyone could truly understand that but my dear Father. You see, I felt hopeless. I was hiding in shame and living in fear. I was a tormented soul who no longer had the will to live. Deep inside, I was screaming. I was ashamed and I hated my reflection. But even still, I knew where to go. He was never far away. I just had to be desperate enough to find Him, and I did.

God is your answer!

Bondage broken

CHAPTER 17

Mercy & Grace

I remember begging for God's grace and begging Him to take all my troubles away. But you see, we already have His grace, His undeserved favor, and it was freely given. Whatever we lack, His grace supplies. God's grace was freely given to me. I had His grace and favor even before I was formed in my mother's womb.

For by grace you have been saved (redeemed and set free) through faith (in Christ). And this is not your own doing; it is the gift of God. Not as a result of works, so that no one may boast. (Ephesians 2:8-9)

I remember asking myself, *Why am I alive?* My mom was in a terrible accident with her friend when she was pregnant with me after driving drunk. She ended up on bedrest for three weeks and then I was born, three months early, and weighing only four pounds. I was on life support for a month. I have always thought, *WOW, I struggled to live even then, someone must have been praying for me. I bet it was a nurse or someone in the ICU who was praying for me.*

One time, I heard God through a preacher, "You were born, because it was God's WILL for YOU to be born – and that's it!!" That was it, so loud and clear. God predestined for me to be born! He had plans for me that no man could take away! The enemy tried, and he tried hard, but to no avail.

I then asked, "Lord, if you are willing, you can make me clean," and He said, "I am willing, be cleansed, daughter."

UNSHAKABLE

Some time after that, I had one of the most prophetic dreams ever. I was wearing a beautiful white wedding dress with no blemishes, just an image of pure beauty and cleanliness. My makeup was beautiful and my hair was done, and I could feel the excitement and nervousness running through my body. I was in the midst of a church and saw people all around, sitting in the pews. They were all staring at me and smiling. I then got the hint and walked down the aisle to the altar. Once at the altar, a priest poured water and anointing oil over my head. In that moment, I felt so blessed, honored, and ordained. I felt so loved while many were watching in awe. It was a glorious revelation, a true daughter of Zion.

You are pure without blemishes, too, because when you are in Christ, you are a bride of Christ and there is no blemish when He sees you. You are made in the likeness and image of God, how could He not love you? You are beautiful and resemble your true Father in heaven. You are worth more than rubies and gold, and most importantly, you are perfect and righteous in Him.

> You are beautiful and resemble your True Father in heaven.

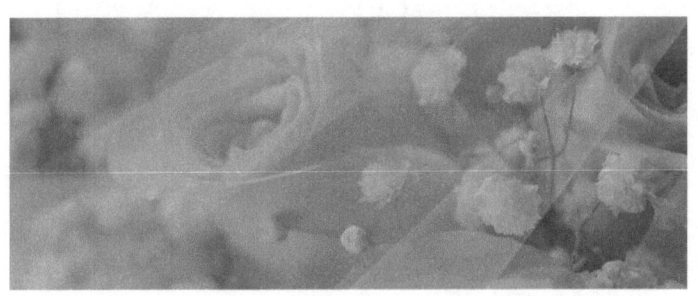

The Bride of Christ

God is your answer!

CHAPTER 18

Big Changes

January 8, 2017, was a cold Monday morning. I walked into my new workplace excited for my journey as a CAD drafter to begin. I can remember the dim narrow hallways. The carpets were old and smelled like they had never been replaced since it was built in the 1960s. Keep in mind that this was an old government building and the air circulation was poor. The offices were small with glass windows; there was an array of them in a rectangular perimeter. I was chaperoned to my office by my new supervisor. She was nice, showed kindness, and had the softest dearest eyes when she looked at me or anyone. The office was bigger. In fact, it was for two. I felt comfortable. That day, I was introduced to one of the most pleasant, welcoming people I have ever met. Her name was "Mer Bear" (Mary) and we are still friends.

Almost instantly, I fit in. I felt like one of those cool kids on a TV sitcom high school show. My real high school years consisted of skipping, smoking weed, and gang activity, so this was definitely a new experience for me. With over 200 employees, a common space, a gym, and various wellness programs, I chose my likings and rolled with it. I made new friends and connected with people and organizations by the numbers. My network grew, as I was going out doing career fairs and STEM (Science, Technology, Engineering, and Math) events, and going to work happy hours.

I took Zumba and chair yoga classes with my coworkers. I grew professionally and began to understand governmental affairs and contracts. I was even sent to company paid trainings. One, called Autodesk University, was in Las Vegas where I met people from all over the world — even a Green Bay Packer fan from Switzerland. That was pretty cool.

I was mountain high and I was free. I got paid a decent income, people liked me, and socially, I was thriving. During those years I sort of forgot about my past. I lived in a nice area and I continued to go to church here and there. Nothing could hold me back!

> I was mountain high and I was free.

Mary and me

God is your answer!

CHAPTER 19

Back to School

I was beginning to get prideful. Even in all this good, my soul wasn't happy. I felt like something was lacking. So to fix this, I decided to go back to school to fulfill an unaccomplished goal, earning a Bachelor's degree. Soon I was in college, taking night classes to pursue a university-level education, all while working full-time. Sometimes my mom would keep the kids overnight, so instead of having to leave work to pick them up and do mom stuff, I could go straight to school after work. She did this for about a year and it really helped me through college.

Ultimately, I worked so hard and kept myself so busy that I didn't take the time for self-care. I submitted myself to every ask. I was doing more for others than I did for myself. Before I knew it, I was juggling too many things at one time. In fact, a counselor at that time told me, "I envision you juggling all these things, and if something gets tossed in the circle, your whole act is going to fall. I don't want to see that happen to you." This was spoken to me at a consultation. Since I didn't think I had time to commit to the counseling, I never returned.

Despite the chaos, I was thriving. I thrived on chaos! Unfortunately, it was during the times of rest, I didn't keep my cool. I was irritable, angry, and not living in the moment. My stress level was high, and I began having anxiety attacks. It got so bad that it began to affect my behavior. I was suffering from headaches and muscle spasms. At first, they were minor, but then they got aggressive to the point that I could physically feel my head tremble.

UNSHAKABLE

I truly believe I opened the door for a spiritual attack during this time. The muscle spasms were on my right side, but the tremors were in the middle of my head where the cerebellum and brain stem meet. The tremors impaired my cognitive thinking and speech, gave me shortness of breath, and tired me out. In fact, I remember passing out at my desk at work. On another occasion, I pulled over and just sobbed in my car, pleading with God once more, "Give me the strength to endure another day!" And He did, time after time, day after day. I put a smile on my face at work, even through the pain — and no one knew.

I saw numerous doctors and specialists including a neurologist. My physical therapist actually felt the tremor and said that in his 30 years of practice, he had never felt anything like that before. He recommended that I go back to the neurologist. So I did. But the doctors came up with nothing and the medication they prescribed did not help. I just endured the pain and prayed every time I felt the onset of symptoms. Prayer helped, but I needed so much more.

Sometimes we can pray and pray and pray and yet still feel nothing. I just wasn't there yet on my journey to know how to declare my healing. I was like the woman in the Bible who suffered from hemorrhages for twelve years and although she spent all she had on physicians, no one could cure her. She went into the crowd seeking the Lord, not caring that she was unclean. She came from behind and touched the hem of Jesus' clothing. She knew she needed a miracle, and He was it. She fought the crowd just to touch a piece of His clothing. And, in so doing, she was healed!

Prayer is powerful, but getting to a place where His presence fills the atmosphere is even more powerful. I needed that! I didn't know what door I had opened for the enemy, but I knew it was time for it to be shut. I couldn't even function anymore and the doctors had no diagnosis. Skeptics may say that it was the stress, and I do believe stress partially had something to do with my pain. But, that was not all. The stress just weakened my ability to fight the attacks from the devil.

> Prayer is powerful, but getting to a place where His presence fills the atmosphere is even more powerful.

At Concordia, where I was taking classes, part of the curriculum was theology. I remember my symptoms worsened during this time. Isn't it a coincidence that this happened at a time of studying God's Word? When I was getting serious about my faith, the attack was magnified. I remember an attack on my birthday. I was watching movies with my family after we had eaten dinner and cake. While I was lying down with the kiddos, I felt the back pain again and the push behind my head. I then felt lightheaded, my vision grew faint, and it was difficult to breathe.

UNSHAKABLE

I knew something was wrong, so I got up from the floor and tried to walk to my room to rest. But as soon as I got up I collapsed. I gathered my strength, walked to my room, and lay down on my bed. By this time my head was pounding. I literally felt my spirit leaving me. It was weird, I felt lifeless as I lay there. I then said boldly, "No, it's not my time. Lord, it is not my time."

I was taken to the emergency room only to be released and sent home after everything checked out okay. The ER doctor said to check in with my primary doctor. So eventually I did, but it was all the same. You are a healthy young lady. I believe they thought I was crazy or something. I wanted to shout something is wrong and you guys can't even figure it out! I was done and irritated. I was weary and worn out. I continued to go to the physical therapist and though it did help relieve some of the symptoms, I continued having those weird tremors.

Graduation from Concordia University

God is your answer!

CHAPTER 20

Set Free

For He says, *When two or more are gathered, He is in the midst.* (Matthew 18:20)

That is just what I needed, prayer warriors praying for me! The doctors were doing nothing, so I took a faith approach. After four years, I was desperate enough to ask for my healing. The people in the discipleship class at Faith Builders Church laid their hands on me and prayed on two occasions. Then the women at the monthly FEW forum encircled me and prayed.

And guess what? One day the tremors were gone! I didn't even notice at first because I had gotten so used to them. I got used to fighting the pain by meditating on scriptures in conjunction with prayers. I felt so liberated and at peace. It was like the scales fell from me and I was finally set free.

We tend to normalize sickness and begin to be okay with illnesses in our bodies. We say things like, "Oh, my diabetes, or, oh my sickness." Guess what? It is not yours! Don't give in to the doctor's report and don't claim the sickness for yourself. I don't care what you have to do, even if you have to crawl into church. Get somewhere where you can be prayed over. Be desperate enough for your healing. Then read and build up your faith and declare your healing every day.

God never intended sickness for us. I have heard so many testimonies of healing, of cancer being eradicated and Alzheimer's being reversed, tumors diminishing, and the list goes on. If you want a powerful book for healing I encourage you to get the book *Eat Your Way to Life and Health* by Joseph Prince.

UNSHAKABLE

God wants us set free. He doesn't want us to live in captivity. People want to blame God, but we need to understand that we live in a fallen world, Satan's playground. But you have the power and authority in Christ to overcome all, because *greater is he that is in you than he that is in the world.* (1 John 4:4)

We don't have to fear Satan and his evil schemes or fall for his lies and deceit, for he has already been defeated. Instead, trust in the Lord and be obedient to him. We can then overcome the powers of darkness and walk boldly in life, unshakable in Him with the power and authority given to us because we are sons and daughters of the most high.

People want to blame God, but we need to understand that we live in a fallen world, Satan's playground.

Set Free in Christ

God is your answer!

CHAPTER 21

God's Gift: Mateo

During the periods of the tremors, I found comfort in drinking socially. For me drinking made the tremors easier to cope with, not to mention it was fun. I also had another problem. I was lonely.

I managed to stay single for two years while pursuing my career and education. When time permitted and the kids were with their dads, I would go out with coworkers. Once, at a margarita happy hour for work, momma had one too many rainbow margaritas and I ended up drunk texting Mario. Can anyone relate? That's all it took! He came over and...whoops, bun in the oven. Just one time; talk about fertile Myrtle! It took a while for Mario to believe the baby was his. He actually didn't believe it until the baby was born. So, I went through most of my pregnancy alone.

He had reason to think it wasn't his. We were not together, so I am sure he must have thought the obvious. But, I know deep in my heart that I kept my side of the street clean. I never doubted. However, it didn't stop the heated arguments and the ridicule that was thrown in my face. I was embarrassed, and more so because people were gossiping that the baby wasn't his.

At work, I pretended that I was still married and that everything was fine at home when in reality I was dying inside from the shame. I only trusted a few people in my circle to tell them what was really going on, and they cared for me, checked on me, and invited me to their special occasions.

UNSHAKABLE

I ended up hiding my pregnancy until I was about 5 or 6 months along because it was easy to hide my tummy in the winter. Once I grew bigger, I believe Mario started to feel compassion for me, and realized that even though we were going through hell, the boys and I shouldn't be alone. So we put our differences aside and I allowed him to come over and see the boys and me.

It was a struggle to have him there when I was scheduled for delivery. I battled with myself and wanted to be selfish, and kept thinking how he didn't deserve this. I was still bitter inside and didn't want to forgive him. I almost prevented him from seeing something so beautiful, the beginning of life, the birthing of his son.

Eventually, I came to my senses. God had forgiven me of all my sins, so why couldn't I forgive this man? Why couldn't I fully surrender to God, to forgive, and let Him deal with Mario's heart and the situation?

K-Love demonstrates this so well on the radio, when they say, "Without love, we are nothing, what good is it to give all our earnings to the poor, but inside we are without love?"

I decided to call Mario at around 8 a.m. to tell him that I was in labor. He showed up around 20 minutes later. The nurses prepared for the birth and began the injection of pitocin. It didn't take long for me to experience the heavy contractions and for my cervix to dilate. My mom was on one side and Mario was on the other. When the time came to push, I remember pushing as hard as I could but I felt very shaky and cold. I was freezing and shivering uncontrollably. None of my other pregnancies felt that way. I thought something was wrong and asked them to warm me up. The nurses brought in warm hot towels which helped a lot.

GOD'S GIFT: MATEO

I remember at one point, the doctor and a resident were having a casual conversation while I was in labor. I wanted to shout, shut up lady, but I didn't. Maybe they did that to distract me. Then finally, after the gushing of blood that frightened my mother and the uncontrollable shivering, Mateo finally came out. That special moment when the baby is all cleaned up and wrapped in the hospital blanket is so sweet. We were filled with joy and couldn't wait to be home.

Mateo's birth was one of my shortest birthing experiences, but it was also the hardest. He resembles that today, so quick-tempered but so loving. He is also very fierce and he defends his bigger brothers. He is four-years-old but will throw a punch in a second if you aren't careful.

In the end, Mateo was just such a little blessing. Immediately, Mario moved back home. I think deep in our hearts we both wanted this. We both needed a change and I believed this was it. We needed our little miracle, Mateo, whose name in Spanish and means gift from God. We settled for a while and the physical abuse stopped. There has not been an incident since the last one in 2017.

I believe Mateo's birth helped us understand that abuse is never right. A man should never touch a woman in anger. However, in our marriage, neither of us was better than the other. I emphasize this because in so many instances we want to blame the other party when, in reality, it's a merry-go-round of childish behavior. One is the enabler, and one is the victim, and then the roles reverse. It is a never-ending journey around the same old mountain until one of the responsible parties decides to put a stop to it. It took us a long time to realize this.

UNSHAKABLE

During the times of my disabling condition, I have to admit that I was irritable and it grew worse. He wasn't around much and when he did come around, we argued about the most childish things ever. We argued about what most couples argue about the dishes, diapers, cleaning, work, bills, etc. We were all grown up now and didn't know how to be collaborating adults. So we argued. He would leave.

I would complain. He would come back smelling like booze, and it went on for some time. I didn't take personal responsibility for my actions and neither did he. I kicked him out again, and that was it. It was easy for me to do that because it was so familiar. I took him back after our third son was born, but ended up leaving him again after about a year.

During all of this, instead of looking in the mirror, I played the victim. I was so angered that nothing good came out of all of it. I couldn't love my husband. I couldn't pray for him. I never had the heart to do so. Our relationship grew cold and I couldn't stand him anymore. He left, and we both dated again, trying to find happiness, but nothing ever filled that void in my heart. Since that dream, I knew exactly what love was and nothing so far had come close, aside from the love of my children. I was content with that, eventually stayed single, and decided to draw closer to God. I wanted a meaningful life – a life of purpose and happiness. This time I was moving two steps ahead instead of one. If I went backward, it was very minor and I got back up quickly because, by this time, I was UNSHAKABLE!

As damaging as this sounds, there is more, so much more. There are untold stories of addiction, lust, generational curses, spiritual warfare, bursts of anger, lies, deceit, and the list goes on. Somehow, we still managed to make it work.

Each of our journeys differed, but we eventually got to the same place of freedom from addiction. We learned to live in freedom; freedom from chains and freedom from bondage. We learned to walk in love, in God's love and put all the trash behind us. We moved from hurt and broken individuals to a life of abundance and joy.

We kept circling the same old mountain from 2017 to 2021 until he gave his life to the Lord in 2023 when he knelt before our King Jesus and let the Holy Spirit get a hold of his life. This happened right before the release of my book, isn't God's timing perfect?!

I will be forever grateful to Pastor Jeff of Faith Builders Church, who played a huge part in this, and to Pastor Hines, CFFC MKE, who told me "Give him to the Lord, it's okay to take your hand off of him, for God says, I got this!"

During all of this, instead of looking in the mirror, I played the victim.

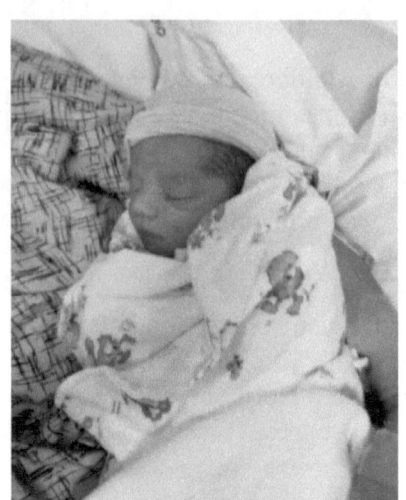

Mateo - God's Gift

Mateo - My mighty warrior

CHAPTER 22

Wisdom and Confidence

Since beginning to work in the construction field in 2020, I have learned so much. I transitioned from a CAD specialist to an engineering aide in construction inspection. While my personal life may have been chaotic and busy, my job is where I soared with wings like eagles. I learned to be confident and stand my ground with such authority.

This was a time in my life when I was physically healed, as mentioned before, and when I spent a lot of time with God praying and worshiping Him on a hilltop surrounding the treatment center where I was working. I prayed as I circled the center sometimes for hours and oftentimes in tears. My heart cried out to God and He heard me. I know He heard because He answered my prayers. For instance, my 96-year-old grandmother, Tota, and I saw my dad become free from a nearly 50-year battle with alcohol addiction. But, most importantly, it was because of this time in prayer that I found my destiny and my purpose in life.

It all started in 2020 when I transitioned from being out in the field, which I loved, to being sent to the treatment plant, which I hated initially. I had a bad attitude about it and was pissed off that I was sent there with such short notice and that my field jobs were taken away abruptly. It was a transition that I was not prepared for. So, when I got to the office and picked my cubicle, I told myself, "I ain't fixing this up, I don't plan on being here long!"

Well, six months went by before I decided to drop the complaining and crappy attitude. I started to admire the place and made all kinds of new friends and acquaintances, specifically males in the trades.

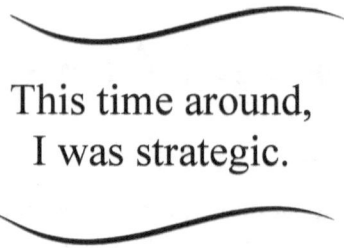

This time around, I was strategic.

I gained confidence and learned how to stand my ground. That didn't mean I wasn't ridiculed behind my back. Actually, I was, and quite often. I chose to ignore it and not let it determine who I was. I had enough of that at my last jobs and knew I wasn't going to let the same old mindsets fool me again.

This time around, I was strategic. I used my femininity in the workplace as a tool for becoming confident and useful in the trade. I learned through questioning and watching, through silence, and through finding a niche of expertise. This is what helped me, but I believe this can help anyone in the career of their choosing.

Questioning is important and I did it wisely. When approaching a job site and meeting the team, I always scoped out each crew member and discerned their character and nature. It didn't take long to figure out who was the lazy one, the apprentice, the chatterbox, the ox, and the pig – like, literally.

The lazy one never has answers, can probably tell you the gist of events, and then goes off on a tangent about their personal lives. The apprentice is learning and is usually quiet, doing the hand-me-down work, but they can be very useful.

They are more inclined to tell you things because they want to be accepted. The chatterbox is the one you want to befriend. This is the one who is going to tell you everything you need to know.

WISDOM AND CONFIDENCE

They pride themselves on teaching and storytelling. The chatterboxes are the people I learned significant amounts of information from and who truly helped me in my inspection career.

The ox is usually the foreman or the guy who has been on the job for more than 20 years and he is normally respected. They know their stuff and they usually don't have time to dumb things down for you. They appreciate the small talk and the minor questions, but don't bother them with much else. It's okay to ask them questions and get clarification, which is vital, but they won't give you a learning experience.

I also learned my job from hands-on-training. I typically stayed and watched while a job got done. I didn't mind asking the crew, "Do you mind if I watch? I have never seen this before and want to learn." In reality, I wasn't asking for their approval, but I was doing this to acknowledge and ask out of courtesy. Learning from a textbook is fine, but you won't get the full effect until you get out there and do it and see it for yourself. You cannot effectively be a project manager unless you get out there and see how exactly a project is done. A doctor cannot give a diagnosis unless he sees and studies the patient's history. A minister cannot minister unless he has people to minister to. My point is that it is critical to get out there in order to do your job effectively.

O that you would be completely silent, And that it would become your wisdom! (Job 13:5)

A fool lets fly with all his temper, but a wise person keeps it back. (Proverbs 29:11)

I don't know about you, but I don't want to be the fool. That is why it is so important to listen!

UNSHAKABLE

Listening brings awareness to all things. It helps discern things; it helps to look from the outside in. As a woman in the trades, I would approach a meeting in silence. Silence is a great strength, it is also wisdom. I didn't speak unless spoken to or until a question arose and I was certain that I knew the definite answer or a meaningful approach. I typically sat behind the scenes and marveled at all the ladies and gents in deep conversation.

What was I doing? I was studying and discerning. I was also using wisdom and knowledge. I didn't feel compelled to just speak because I was the only woman, or because I needed to prove my worth. I know that I am worthy, wise, and confident. I know that I don't know all things and I don't pretend to. I know that I can ask questions and give helpful advice when needed.

I chose to learn through a healthy balance of silence. I also ensured I was well prepared. That means if you have to create your own homework during off hours, then do so. This is going to help in the long run. It doesn't take much while waiting in line to open your phone and watch a YouTube video on a topic instead of lurking around on social media.

This brings me to the next suggestion for finding your niche for the present. Find that one thing that just makes you tick, the thing that you can study and master. I found mine in the trades and it made me that much more valuable.

Before I knew it, I was being invited to meetings that were not my concern. I sat in on meetings during the design phase, not only during the construction phase. The knowledge I gained was vital for million-dollar contracts in the design and pilot phases. They wanted me on the job. Why? Because I learned, I did my homework and ensured I was always there on the job to see how it got done.

WISDOM AND CONFIDENCE

So many of us just want to do the minimum and then go home. So many people have excuses and complaints. Then they wonder why they get passed up for a promotion, or why they can never be happy. So many of us just want to throw a pity party and say, "Why me? Why me? Life isn't fair!"

Well, guess what, life isn't fair! This is why the Bible says, *The harvest is plenty, but the workers are few.* (Matthew 9:37-38) Be one of the few! Listen, if I did it with three children as a full-time student and worker, leaving an abusive relationship and as a single mom, all while battling anxiety, tension, muscle spasms, and fatigue, then you can do it, too! I laugh because I remember doing homework at 10:00 and 11:00 at night while my right hand or foot was rocking my baby to sleep in his bouncer. I may have looked crazy, but I got the job done and graduated at the top of my class, and you can do it, too.

You are not weak, you are strong! When you do feel weak, give the Lord your human weakness in exchange for His supernatural strength.

People ask me all the time, "How did you do it?" I say, "God." There is no other explanation. Those weary days on my way home from work when I would just cry in my car, God was there, He hugged me and imparted His strength into me. He was my strength each day and night. You can't tell me there is no God!

I have seen manifestation after manifestation over and over. I have heard and felt His presence. I have seen confirmations through dreams, through His Word, and through people. I have seen signs, wonders, and miracles happen in my life, and they continue to this day. If He did it for me, then He can do it for you. But first, there needs to be a shaking in your life, so that you can become UNSHAKABLE!

UNSHAKABLE

Begin to rebuild the mighty walls once again, but this time on a firm foundation in Him, in faith, in His Word, and through the storms. The storms make us stronger, so when the storm comes, be a bull who runs toward it ready to get through it, instead of a cow who musters all its strength to run from it, then grows weary because the storm continues chasing it.

That is how I got through this era of my life as a Latina construction inspector, bold and fierce because the righteous are bold like a lion.

Pops and me fully restored

Rossie - Construction Inspector

Prayer Warring

God is your answer!

CHAPTER 23

Walking Like David

I felt like a warrior, like David! As I marched down the roadway to face the enemy, I imagined my very steps shaking the earth. I closed my eyes and prayed. *Lord! Help me, give me strength. Give me the right words to speak!* As I opened my eyes, I saw a hawk, beautifully flying with wings wide open. I didn't have to see a hawk to know that God was with me. I knew He was. This symbol was confirmation that God was caring for me and diligently watching over His offspring (me).

That Day!

It was a normal Thursday, can't-wait-for-Friday kind of day. My work phone chirped. I got a message from an unknown number and flipped it open without thinking. On the screen was an image that made me gasp. Chills ran down my back. Who was this and why were they sending me a picture of an erect penis? I quickly closed the phone, embarrassed, and for some reason, ashamed. Hundreds of thoughts went through my mind. I relived that very moment from my childhood when I asked myself, "Why did he do that, am I a disgusting little girl?" I was a resident inspector for multiple jobs, so it isn't out of the ordinary that contractors have my number. I thought to myself, *Is this a random person with a wrong number or did the pervert actually know me?*

For some reason, I decided to text back and say, "Wrong number." Of all the things I could have said, and wished, for that matter, I didn't. I simply said, "Wrong number," and carried on. Ding! Another message came through. This time I didn't open it, I just read the headline asking if they could do the unspoken to me. How did they know I was a woman?

UNSHAKABLE

I began to think, *Was it someone I knew?* Still, I ignored it and carried on with my work. The messages continued until 4:00 p.m. Did someone know my workday ended at 4:00 p.m.? I began to feel fearful and watched very carefully as I pulled out of the secure gated area of the treatment plant. I thought maybe I should go to headquarters downtown and turn the phone in and tell them this disturbing news. And then I didn't; I just carried on and went home.

Accusations

The next day, I didn't get any texts. I thought, *Okay it's over, they got tired and decided to quit. It was probably a wrong number or spam.* We had about five different contractors working for us that day. I kept busy and tried to go about my day, but every time I stood in front of one of the contractors, that image flashed through my mind and I thought, *Was it him?* I even glanced at the arms, because I remembered that the person was hairy and fair-skinned. Then I thought, *Stop being ridiculous.*

At the end of the day, there was one contractor who was still working, a quiet fella who usually kept to himself. A few months back, his cousin passed away, so I shared the gospel with him, and he showed responsiveness. Up until now, our talks had been small talk, nothing major, so I didn't think anything of it or him. I didn't even stare at him like I did the others. That Friday at 4:00 p.m. he asked if he could work on Saturday to finish this job because he was not going to be in on Monday. I made a quick call to the construction manager who said he could if I would be willing to check in on him. I asked the contractor to please make sure to sign the daily work permit because I had not received one from him on Friday. He said, "I apologize, next time I will."

At 5:00 p.m., I got a message from the pervert. I thought, God, I feel tormented, what is going on?

But it was Friday and I had things to do, so I shut the phone off and ignored it.

Saturday

Early Saturday afternoon, I checked on the contractor who was working that day. We made small talk and then I left. Not too long after there was a ding signaling another text message. It was THAT number! I thought to myself, This is really weird, how do they know I have the phone on me? An hour later the contractor texted me stating that he was done working for the day. I didn't respond. I was already irritated.

On Monday, I received another message from the number, this time at 6:00 a.m. Again, I didn't open it, I just read the headline. The first line that popped up was, "I Apologize." In that instant, I knew who it was. I didn't say anything, as I had never opened any of the messages since the day of the picture when I responded, "Wrong number." I had been silent this entire time, praying to God that they would be exposed.

The Battle!

The whole week was silent, the contractor was not onsite. However, he did send a random message to my work phone over the next weekend asking, "Hey, do you have the kids?" I never responded. Monday came, and I got a message in the morning from the contractor at 6:00 a.m. saying "Oh, I am sorry that message was not for you, I accidentally sent it to the wrong person."

To be clear, I never did get any more messages from the anonymous pervert. Work was being done at the bottom of the hill that day, and I fought myself, thinking, I don't want to see him. I just won't go down there today. I almost gave up and let the enemy win, and then I remembered: The Armor of God.

UNSHAKABLE

Finally, be strong in the Lord and in his mighty power. Put on the full armor of God, so that you can take your stand against the devil's schemes. For our struggle is not against flesh and blood, but against the rulers, against the authorities, against the powers of this dark world, and against the spiritual forces of evil in the heavenly realms. Therefore put on the full armor of God, so that when the day of evil comes, you may be able to stand your ground, and after you have done everything, to stand. Stand firm then, with the belt of truth buckled around your waist, with the breastplate of righteousness in place, and with your feet fitted with the readiness that comes from the gospel of peace. In addition to all this, take up the shield of faith, with which you can extinguish all the flaming arrows of the evil one. Take the helmet of salvation and the sword of the Spirit, which is the word of God.

And pray in the Spirit on all occasions with all kinds of prayers and requests. With this in mind, be alert and always keep on praying for all the Lord's people. (Ephesians 6:11-18)

I began to walk down that hill as if I was shaking the earth with every step, with every breath. And he saw me! I could see his car in the distance, as he quickly got in and sat in it. As I got closer, he turned on the engine and drove around the corner. I chuckled. He then came back and parked, got out, and walked towards the piping that he was supposed to have worked on hours ago. I approached him and said, "Why haven't you worked on this?" Without making eye contact, he said, "I was taking measurements from inside the building." I said, "Oh that's funny, that shouldn't have taken you that long." He said, "Okay, well I will start this portion of insulation right now."

Before I walked away, I did a slight turn, and looking at his troubled, nervous, shameful eyes, I said, "What's with your text message from Saturday?"

WALKING LIKE DAVID

He said, "Oh sorry that was a mistake, wrong person." Sound familiar? I said, "You sure about that?" He moved the cigarette from his face, his expression changed, and in that moment he let out a guilty but offended expression and said, "Yeah." It wasn't the kind of gesture that most people would make when they say they are innocent. It was the kind that tried to deny it all. His "yeah" spoke volumes, like how dare you accuse me? What would he have been accused of? A harmless message that wasn't meant for me, or an act of perversion that stemmed from a thought and manifested itself to reality?

After his "yeah" I said, "This is a work phone, it is a government phone, be careful with what you do because I am going to turn it in."

He shook his head in agreement, head still down. I almost walked away, then I turned and said, "You need to seek GOD." Again he nodded. I walked away with my head held high, a smile on my face and with the power that was given to me by my Heavenly Father to face the enemy and shame him. And I did shame him. My presence alone shamed him.

I love what David said and it makes me chuckle because I think to myself, I could have used his line. *For who is this uncircumcised Philistine, that he should defy the armies of the living God.* (1 Samuel 7:26)

He defiled me and thought it was okay, but little did he know, this young woman who spent time praising God and talking to God alone on a mountaintop would be the one to put him in his place. She would be the one to shame the devil because we do not wrestle against flesh and blood, but against the rulers, against the authorities, against the powers of this dark world, and against the spiritual forces of evil in the heavenly realms.

Soaring high with wings like eagles

CHAPTER 24

The Journey

Even in the aftermath of this incident, I loved being at the treatment center. I loved it so much and I enjoyed learning so many great things from the people I worked with. We created meaningful relationships. Most were receptive to my faith. Others just liked someone who had a listening ear. I was that person, their person when they felt hopeless and hurt, or when they felt happy and talkative. My excitement and happiness were contagious and affected most people I came into contact with.

I did my job exceedingly well, but I also had time to spend with my heavenly Father. I would take long walks and just talk to Him. Have you ever just enjoyed a walk in nature and just talked to the Creator? Well, I did, and it was beautiful. This was my quiet time to pray and to praise.

Did you know He loves that? It's the quality of time spent in a relationship that is so important. People don't understand that the Lord desires to have quality time with you and that you can speak to Him at any moment of the day. People run away from Christianity because of the religion and ceremonial laws, and mostly because of other Christians. But the Lord didn't come for that. The Pharisees and religious Jews even persecuted him for hanging out with basically what society calls the "scum of the earth."

It is not those who are well who need a physician, but those who are sick. (Luke 5-31)

UNSHAKABLE

I sure was one of them, one of the "scums of the earth." I hate to say it that way, but that is what people viewed me as; they even said I was "garbage." But the Lord said I am his treasure. Some people hate me today and I have no recollection of them. They hate me and I don't even know them. Someone said, "It's because of your past, who you hung out with, and what you stood for. You offended many people."

Wow, just WOW! I want to say that I am sorry, truly sorry to anyone whom I may have hurt in my past. I was naïve and ignorant and was dealing with so much hate, anger, and hurt. That does not permit me to do such things. But I have come to a place where I have given it all to God and I am now forgiven of it all. I am living a clean and righteous slate.

On the contrary, some people will hate you for just being YOU. They hate positivity, and they hate people who always see the light and optimistic view. You can be living in darkness and be called the black sheep of the family. You could be getting your life back together, and someone has something to say about that, and how it won't last. You could be doing exceedingly well and now people murmur, "Oh, they used to be this or that, and now they think they are greater." You can give your life to Jesus, and love Him with all your heart, and people will say, "Oh, so and so turned religious, and think they are perfect."

My point is that people are always going to judge you and have something to say. Don't feel angered when this happens, because it is impossible that offense will not come. Continue to transform and don't give in to hypocrisy. Bless them anyway. This is heavy material, but you need to hear it because we all need Jesus. He loves us dearly. He loved me even on my worst day. You see, none of us are worthy on our own.

THE JOURNEY

We are only worthy through his son, Jesus Christ, because He lived a sinless life and died for me and you. Because of Him, I have God's grace and mercy, and where I lack, His grace supplies. It is a gift that meets all my needs.

And when I fall short, and when I stumble, He is there. This is when I get even closer to him instead of condemning myself. We won't get it right 100% of the time. Sometimes we cave in to temptation and mess things up. It's okay; God knows our hearts. God knows all things from the beginning to the end. God knew that I would fall into drugs and alcohol time and time again. He knew I would falter into anger and infidelity. He knew I would deal with lust and homosexuality, and he loved me even still. He continued to love a wretch like me and he has never forsaken me. God doesn't count righteousness by how perfect we are, he counts righteousness by how many times we fall and get back up.

He loves you now more than ever, just the way you are. All we have to do is give our hearts to Him and let Him do the rest. Let Him clean out your heart. I ask Him every day,

Will you let Him heal your heart?
Will you let Him patiently remove the things that don't belong?

UNSHAKABLE

Renew in me a clean heart O God; and renew a right spirit within me. (Psalm 51:10)

Will you let Him heal your heart? Will you let Him patiently remove the things that don't belong? Believe me, I get better and better every year. He is working on me, and I am still a work in progress.

My journey taking a discipleship class at my local church (Faith Builders Spring of 2021), finding the Christian Women's group called "FEW" which stands for the Fellowship of Extraordinary Women (2021 Sept. Conference), going back to school, and being positioned at the South Shore Water Treatment facility where I felt like I was sojourning in the desert, was no coincidence. I was being prepared for so much more in a very short span of time. I was now in my 30s, and it was time to grow up, both spiritually and mentally. It was time to put the childish behavior away and become everything God has purposed for me. I was able to find my real purpose and calling during this period of my life.

What is my purpose in life? It is the power of exhortation, to pull people forward, be encouraging, and to talk and spread joy and laughter. My uncle (R.I.H) saw it in me at the age of six. He told Momma, "That girl is beautiful, and she is going to be great and so lifegiving."

I have been CALLED. God woke me up one night in his audible voice and spoke to me. I felt scared and unworthy to be called, but His voice was bold and powerful. His voice was great and affirming, His voice was a father's voice telling me exactly what I needed to do. I felt like Moses. I was sent by God, not on my own authority, but by his authority. I do not glorify myself, but He that has sent me to do his work. I am his faithful servant, and I am called even when I don't feel qualified.

THE JOURNEY

It happened in the spring of 2021 around the season of Passover. I knew right then and there that it was time to get to work. Although, I reasoned with God and said, "Okay Lord, if You want me to do this, then You are going to have to show me how and put the right people in my path." Then I chuckled with God.

And he did. He put plenty there throughout the years.

Food for thought: Don't think of God as this angered man who pours wrath on the earth. He is precious, life-giving, merciful, and gracious and loves like a father. If he corrects your bad habits, just remember, He is loving you like a father. That's what fathers do. They correct their children in all love. They want you to be all that is destined for you.

I have had numerous dreams of Him and in each dream, He was holding my hand. I could see my small hand in His and then He would squeeze it and lift it up. In other dreams, I was hugging him so tightly. I couldn't see His face, only the outline of His body.

He let me just embrace Him, and in that moment I felt so secure and loved. He surely does return to you the years that have been eaten (robbed) by the locust. He did this for me on a spiritual level and in the natural sense with my earthly father. He is the God of restoration. But, that is a story for another book!

God is your answer!

Finding FEW

CHAPTER 25

The Shift into My Assignment

I ultimately left my secured construction job to walk into my new calling. I knew I was doing the right thing because God specifically called me to it, and if *God is for you then who can be against you.* (Romans 8:31) I stand tall and firm knowing that I am in His perfect will, for He is for me. Whenever doubt tries to creep in, I remember all the doors He opened along the way and all the people He put into my path. I remember all the triumphs and victories, especially the answered prayers. I thank God that I am healed and on my path to greatness doing even greater things and assignments that I have never imagined that I could do.

I look back and marvel at all the attempts Satan had on my life. Ever since I was born, he has tried to take me out, from infancy and innocence, to adolescence, and into adulthood. But, God! He has the last word and never loses a battle. And when He called, I answered.

It was the spring of 2022, and a new position had opened up at my workplace that I was qualified for and it paid such a great salary. I had thought about applying, but immediately (internally) I turned it down because I knew the Lord had other plans for my life. I knew this because I received confirmation from a prophetic speaker the past winter. During the previous six months, people who were close to me personally and professionally also confirmed this. It was now a matter of time. It was God's prompting season and I just needed patience.

UNSHAKABLE

Unfortunately, I somehow got sidetracked and was deceived into applying for the position. I began to reason with myself and the person who wanted me to apply. I was convinced that I was making the right choice and that I deserved this position.

That was a mistake! I knew the truth, I discerned it, but did it anyway.

I did not put my full trust in God in this matter. Sorry, Lord.

I ended up applying and went through the interview process. Weeks passed by and I heard nothing, just silence. I began to have a gut-wrenched feeling and no longer felt confident that the job was mine.

One Friday, I went home, sat on my couch, and thought about the job. Just then, in the silence of my home, I felt the Holy Spirit impress upon my heart and whisper, "It's not yours."

I texted Momma Kim, as I sat in the living room, enveloped by the dim lighting. She was kind and said, "Guess what honey, how do you get to the place of destiny? By getting a lot of NOs — it's a pathway of yes and no bricks."

It was exactly what I needed to hear. It's like God was preparing me for the NO even before it happened. That's just like Him though, preparing the way, even when I messed up. I ended up getting the NO a few weeks later, and the thank you response from HR.

I did feel humiliated as my co-workers knew I had applied for the position. My thought process was, "I will just be out of here before the new employee starts." Realistically, I did not want to meet the person who took my job. So again, I reasoned with myself and took matters into my own hands, and began to apply at other organizations.

THE SHIFT INTO MY ASSIGNMENT

One organization called me and asked me to interview. To my surprise, I crushed it. The hiring manager was so inspired by me. She offered me the position, but there was a problem. It was a 9-5 position making $10 less an hour than what I was currently making. My heart, even while wanting to go, just couldn't. I knew it wasn't the time.

Then the Lord gave me a dream. He loves to talk to me through dreams.

And in that dream, I was in that position and when I saw myself in the dream I looked so burnt out. I had lots of gray hair and I looked so tired.

Finally, I walked in obedience and didn't take it. I turned it down and waited for the day that the new employee started. The day finally came, the day I met the woman who took my position. I was eager to look her in the eyes to see just how confident and impressive she was. I imagined a beautiful blonde with flowing hair and a nice figure. Needless to say, she was quite different. She was a very simple and happy human being who loved nature and who knew absolutely nothing about construction. She was a cute kid who definitely needed a mentor. And, I was that mentor for her!

The next couple of months she became a close coworker. We did our walks around the treatment plant and just talked. Sometimes we talked about religion because she said she was an atheist. Sometimes we talked about politics, and sometimes about music, art, and dance. She had her point of view and I had mine. And we shared them so respectfully.

UNSHAKABLE

We even talked about deep things, about healing from the wounds of our past. She even entrusted me with some of her most vulnerable personal stories. I began to feel bad; bad about judging her, bad about getting offended. One day I said to her, "Hey, I've got to tell you something." She said, "Sure." I told her that I had applied for her position and didn't get it. She said she knew, but didn't know the whole story.

We then talked about it, dismissed it, and carried on. The walks continued, and the summer came. It was a good season. But my time there was finally coming to an end. I was being transitioned to another place. A place that could no longer work for me on a personal level. **My wilderness was coming to an end.**

I knew moving to another location meant more freeway time, odd hours, and later start and end times. I had experienced that at my other job and hated long freeway commutes, especially to the other side of town. It also meant less time to see my kids. My three-year-old would be starting half-day K3 that year and then be transported to a daycare, so being that far away was not an option for me.

I just knew, **NOW** was the time to go. It was God's prompting season. He nudged my heart and knowing God's Word, He said you can be angry now (for there is a righteous anger that we can have, but sin not). As I took my final walks at the treatment plant, I knew it was a release of all that frustration, and the Lord knew this. He understood and allowed me to pack my bags and go in peace. Like a cloud by day I moved, and we moved together.

I knew that I wanted to work on my business plan and open my coaching business in the fall. Thankfully, after all that, I was still on track. I prayed about it and asked God, "When God, when?

THE SHIFT INTO MY ASSIGNMENT

Sometimes God lets us choose the little details. We don't need to overcomplicate things. We are still adults and can make decisions for ourselves.

So, I chose the first day of August. In doing that, I heard a message about how Abraham left his kindred at God's appointed time. Abraham didn't know where he was to go. He had to leave everything that seemed so familiar to him and obey God. God said to leave, and so he did without knowing where he was going to go.

I was fearful, but I knew I was in His will and would be okay. So I left, without knowing where I was going to go. I put in my notice on Friday, July 15, 2022. That night, I went to a Women's Circle meeting. The meeting ended and I left. While driving home, I got a call from the facilitator of the meeting. She was really excited and told me to turn around and come back, which I did. The executive director of the ministry that hosted the women's circle meeting said they were in need of a case manager for their pantry. He said he was interested in me and to call him for an interview.

The following week, I called and left a message, then followed up with an email. When he and his wife got back from vacation, he gave me a call. It was meant to be. I was everything they were looking for. I started in August, familiarizing myself with the company and community agencies. I began case management services in September at the Wednesday Food Pantry from 9:00-11:30 a.m. and it was a total success. I reached so many people who needed to be loved and cared for! They needed to be fed and clothed both spiritually and naturally. In fact, we use this verse for the people,

Man does not live on bread alone. Rather he lives on every word that comes from the mouth of God (Matthew 4:4)

UNSHAKABLE

We give them bibles (both Spanish and English) and we clothe them. The pantry gives them food and resources. Auntie Chris and I pray for them, we comfort them. We strengthen their spirits with God's words. We set the captives free. And today, my promises are this,

I am a mother of hope.
A mother to the needy,
and a mother to the prisoners.

I am able to reach people through my business, ministry, and on social media. It is a new adventure, a different platform, and exciting to just trust God through it all! Being able to take people to their next journey in life and aiding them through alignment is so fulfilling because life is a journey and no one should have to do it alone.

This happened because I said yes; yes to my destiny, yes to God's work, yes to happiness, and most importantly, yes to healing and obedience. Taking the risk is the first step because knowing that you are in God's will is the safest place to be. He created us to be unique masterpieces, all with our own individual callings. So if you don't know yours, then maybe you haven't asked Him yet. I encourage you to seek, ask, knock. Spend time in prayer and in His Word. Find like-minded women who will empower you.

That's what I did. I never knew it was so easy. The challenging part is obeying God during His prompting and doing it His way Then you will not be circling the mountain time and time again and you will do what you were made for. Waiting on God's timing is the best thing you can do. I finally did, and I don't regret one thing because if I saved one life, then it was worth every penny, and I would do it again. Even our maker leaves the 99 to find just one. And that one could be you.

THE SHIFT INTO MY ASSIGNMENT

I want you to be set free, total freedom. Yes, God heard my cries, but that doesn't mean I was living the best life. I could have figured it out sooner, but because I was ignorant, disobedient, and lacked knowledge, I missed out on a lot of opportunities and went through things that I didn't have to go through. Thank the Lord that I survived and went from surviving to thriving.

Here are some verses that I like to meditate on. They remind me so much of my life.

Come and hear, all you who fear God (reverencing the Lord, the beginning of wisdom)
and I will tell you what he has done for my soul.
I cried to him with my mouth,
And high praises on my tongue,
If I had cherished iniquity (sin) in my heart
The Lord would not have listened;
He has attended to the voice of my prayer.

Blessed be God,
Because he has not rejected my prayer
Or removed his steadfast love from me! (Psalm 66:16-20)

Wow! I still get choked up with this, because I never meant to disappoint him, I was only hurting inside and found unhealthy ways to cope. Even still, because I did not cherish the inequity, he listened to my prayers and never shut me out. He never gave up on me and he won't give up on you.

So I thank you for allowing me to share my success story, along with the tears and my soul poured into this. If I struggled to survive the first 33 years of my life, can you imagine what God can do with the rest of it? I am all in and fully surrendered to His will, for look what the Lord has done. I hope I inspired you to be the unique masterpiece of yourself! Because you truly are one.

UNSHAKABLE

My hope is that you use this book as a blueprint for healing, resiliency, and overcoming darkness. Or maybe you are thriving in Christ and found this book inspiring for others. Then I would challenge you to share this book with someone who is hurting or someone who is broken, someone who feels hopeless and lost, or someone who is holding onto a mustard seed of faith by a thread. Because a mustard seed of faith can move mountains, and it surely did for me when I was in the infancy stage of Christianity and even when I fell time and time again. We can combat negativity, unbelief, suicidal thoughts, depression, anger, hopelessness, insecurity, shame, guilt, and the list goes on. We can combat that through His word and promises, and being led by the Holy Spirit.

Who is God to me?

He is my everlasting Father (Isaiah 9:6)
He is my healer (Psalms 103:3)
He is my redeemer (Isaiah 59:20)
He is my deliverer (Psalms 70:5)
He is my strength (Psalms 43:2)
He is my shelter (Joel 3:16)
He is my friend (John 15:15)
He is my advocate (1 John 2:1)
He is my restorer (Psalms 23:3)
He is love (1 John 4:16)
He is my mediator (1 Timothy 2:5-6)
He is my stronghold (Nahum 1:7)
He is the bread of life (John 6:35)
He is my hiding place (Psalms 32:7)
He is the everlasting light (Isaiah 60:20)
He is a strong tower (Proverbs 18:10)
He is my resting place (Jeremiah 50:6)

THE SHIFT INTO MY ASSIGNMENT

He is the spirit of truth (John 16:13)
He is my refuge from the storm (Isaiah 25:4)
He is eternal life (1 John 5:20)
He is the Lord who provides (Genesis 22:14)
He is the Lord of peace (2 Thessalonians 3:16)
He is the living water (John 4:10)
He is my shield (Psalms 144:2)
He is my helper (Hebrews 13:6)
He is my wonderful counselor (Isaiah 9:6)
He is the Lord who heals (Exodus 15:26)
He is my hope (Psalms 71:5)
He is the God of comfort (Romans 15:5)

This is my list. Who is God to you?

I hope you will help someone else when you come to the realization of who our perfect Father really is. I hope that if you are healed and thriving, you will consider who you can bless today. Finally, I hope you found this book uplifting and a form of healing for whatever you are going through because nothing is impossible for God.

For the LORD has anointed me to bring good news to the poor. He has sent me to comfort the brokenhearted and to proclaim that captives will be released and prisoners will be freed. (Isaiah 61:1)

With God anything is possible.

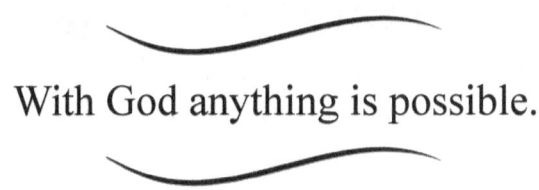

With God anything is possible.

Our little happy family

My Milwaukee family

Auntie Chris at the Food Pantry

Brooke and me serving at the Food Pantry

God is your answer!

Community Organizations

ALMA Center
Non-Profit Organization
https://almacenter.org/
Phone: 414-265-0100
2821 N. Vel Phillips Ave., Third Floor
Milwaukee, WI 53212
The Alma Center works to heal, transform, and evolve the unresolved pain of trauma that fuels the continuation of cycles of violence, abuse, and dysfunction in families and communities. We work primarily with at-risk men or those in the criminal justice system with a particular focus on men who have a history of domestic violence.

Bizstarts Institute
President: Patrick Snyder
Website: www.bizstarts.com
Phone: 414-973-2334
Services: FREE Complimentary Entrepreneurial Coaching and Community Support

Blossoming Rubies
Owner: LaWanda Redmond
Contact: (LaWanda) 414-530-7481 & (Lesa) 414-218-2061
Mission: Safe Space for Girls to Be Rubies
Youth programming for girls 13 - 17 years old

City On A Hill
Non-Profit Organization
2224 W. Kilbourn Ave.
Milwaukee, WI 53233
Mission: City on a Hill transforms cities and families by restoring hope, enhancing the quality of life, and advancing justice for all generations.
Website: www.cityonahill.org

Defy Ventures EIT Program & UWM EXT
Website: www.go.wisc.edu/EITpartnership
Facebook: www.facebook.com/eitpartnership
Education & Support For Justice Impacted Individuals
Services: Entrepreneur Bootcamp Training and Acceleration Courses

Ebenezer Stone West - Food Pantry Services
1127 S. 35th St. (behind church, bring ID)
Milwaukee, WI 53214
Wednesday 9:00am - 11:30am
Saturday 9:00am - 11:30am

FEW-The Fellowship of Extraordinary Women
Founder and Champion of women: Kimberly Joy
Website: www.thefewwomen.com
Mission: FEW awakens, activates, and accelerates women in their Divine destinies in Christ. FEW accelerates extraordinary in faith, family, and business.
Services: FEW offers membership, publishing services, and three certifications: FEW Leadership, FEW Institute of Trainers, and FEW Confident Keynote Speaking.

FREE
C3 & C4 Organization
www.freemvmnt.org
Facebook: Free - Reclaiming Women's Freedom
Mission: The FREE Campaign is focused on the unique issues of women who have experienced incarceration.
Services: Women Support Circles and Advocacy

Geno's Pantry & Adoration Abode (Watertown Milwaukee)
Owner: Anne Schmidt
Contact: 920-342-2032
Website: https://www.adorationabode.com/
Mission: Adoration Abode is a 501(c)(3) organization bringing resources to those who need them.

From providing transitional housing at the House of Hope, supplementing a family's food resources from Geno's Pantry, providing a home-cooked meal from Meal of Hope, to experiencing fellowship and a sense of community at The Hope Outreach Center. Together we can meet the needs of our community.

Healing Hearts
Owner: Nilda Andaverd
Email: healingheartsbynilda@gmail.com
Text: 262-271-6726
Mission: Healing hearts through active listening and gentle guiding sessions to release the bonds that keep us trapped in the past.
Si Habla Espanol

Inflight Coaching & Ministry Services
Owner: Linnea West
Website: https://www.inflightservices.net
linnea.inflight.services@gmail.com
Call: 262-893-3869
Mission: Soar Higher & Change Your Destiny
Contact Linnea for a free consultation

Journey2Alignment Coaching
Owner: Rossie Manka
Website: www.journey2alignmentcoaching.com
Email: journey2alignment414@gmail.com
Mission: To Empower Women to be the Unique Masterpiece of Herself through coaching, mentoring, and ongoing support.
We also specialize in technology coaching, group coaching, women support circles, and entrepreneur coaching for all.
Call for a free consultation

National Domestic Violence Hotline
Hours: 24/7.
Languages: English, Spanish, and 200+ through interpretation service
800-799-7233

Need a good church?
Faith Builders Church MKE
4901 S. Howell Ave., Milwaukee, WI.
Visit In-Person or Online

Reality Check By Kim
email:realitycheckbykim@gmail.com
Call: 262-225-8479
Youth Programming
Parent and Student Counseling
About: Kim is a retired parole and probation officer who now educates students about the reality of the criminal justice system. She also informs parents about social media safety and security.

Re'Zilyent Mke Inc.
Owner: LaWanda Redmond
Website: https://www.rezilyentmke.com/
Contact: 414-218-2061
Re'Zilyent Consultant aids in affordable housing and supportive services.
Our vision is to see individuals simply move forward while remaining resilient through providing affordable housing and supportive services.

Share the Love Ministries
Owner: Veronica Stanton
Contact: info@sharetheloveinc.com
Mission: Share the Love is committed to empowering Milwaukee's community by providing comprehensive support services fostering intimate healing relationships.

Our mission is to meet individuals where they are, without judgment, and help them elevate their circumstances, ensuring a safer, more inclusive environment for all.

Sojourner Family Peace House
Non-Profit Organization
619 W. Walnut
Milwaukee, WI 53212
Website: https://www.familypeacecenter.org/
24-hour hotline & crisis shelter:
Call: 414-933-2722
Text: 414-877-8100
Sojourner provides an array of support to nearly 8,000 clients each year aimed at helping families affected by domestic violence achieve safety, justice, and well-being.

Suicide & Crisis Lifeline
Call 988 or visit www.988lifeline.org
Suicide prevention and help: www.rehma.org

Team Havoc
Rafael Mercardo
Facebook: Team Havoc
Emergency Narcan Administration, community walks, and prayer at the park

Unspoken w/Candace Sanchez
Owner: Candace Sanchez
Contact: candaceshanchez.com
Mission: We are about healing, encouragement, and support. And, with that in mind, trust that there is power in speaking your truth and sharing your experiences with others because you can change and save someone's life. We advocate for victims of sexual violence and abuse.

Community Recognition

To Sydney: *Honey you are beautiful, you touch my heart with* your stories. You love to camp and sit out and watch the stars. In winter you are cold and I want to remind you to take care of yourself. Please get to a shelter and don't forget to continue writing in your notebooks. I pray God uses your writing to touch so many. And when the time comes, I pray that you are ignited and soaring like an eagle.

To Lydia: You are precious and loving. Even though you struggle, you always find ways to smile and help others in need. When I gave you that belt, you laughed and put it on saying, "I feel secure." The Lord, in that moment, gave me a revelation concerning you. You are his mighty warrior secured in Him. Keep pressing on. In Him, you are made new. Love you, Sweetheart.

To Lisa: God's sojourner. Though you go from place to place, God is with you. He is with you in times of trouble and He continues to be your help. You are His, don't ever forget that. You can call upon Him and He is there for you. I pray blessings over you and your child and your children's children. Remember what we talked about. When you feel the temptations, stop and pray and give it to the Lord. Victory is yours.

To Deborah: You have such childlike faith. And it works! I am so glad God brought your cat, Squirrely, back to you. The Lord truly does listen to His children. I am blessed to know that you finally found shelter. May you always find shelter and most importantly, shelter in the Lord.

To all the kind people at the pantry: You have always blessed me with your raw and real conversations and given me the privilege to pray for you. I will always have a special place in my heart for all of you: Mike, Robin, Mikey, the volunteers, Mrs. B., Maria, Dalia, Rosamaria, Irma, Rebbeca, Michelle, Natasha, Alysha, Deborah, Anne, Brooke, Mark, Mike, Sandy, Jackie, Larry, Phillip, Thomas, Maria, Harry, Yolanda & Luisa, and the list goes on.

About the Author

Rossie Manka is living her purpose and passion as an author, motivational speaker, certified coach and trainer. She is a former civil engineer technician and construction inspector where she broke barriers as a female in a male-dominated field.

Rossie's desire to move people forward goes beyond a vision. It is her call to action! As a justice-impacted individual and enthusiastic entrepreneur, she knows the importance of giving back to her community in the form of ministry, education, and outreach.

Rossie founded Journey2Alignment Coaching Services in 2022 with a vision to see *Happy and Healthy Individuals Healed and On Their Path to Greatness.*

Rossie enjoys an adventurous life with her husband and sons in Milwaukee, Wisconsin. With three young boys, there's never a dull moment. Rossie and her family especially love trying new restaurants. At her sons' request, Rossie created her own restaurant rating system. She now considers herself an amateur food critic. Follow Rossie on socials or contact her for a free consultation.

Facebook: Journey 2 Alignment Coaching Service LLC
LinkedIn: Rossie Manka
Website: journey2alignmentcoaching.com
Email: journey2alignment414@gmail.com

FEW International Publications
An Extraordinary Publishing Experience

FEW International Publications is a #1 Bestselling Publisher for women authors at all levels who are seeking more from telling their stories than just a printed project. We are privileged to watch FEW Authors connect, learn, grow, and heal through the creation of a written work that impacts others and glorfies God. Find FEW's books at thefewwomen.com and on amazon.com.

Extraordinary Women, Extraordinary Stories

#AccelerateExtraordinary

thefewwomen.com

www.ingramcontent.com/pod-product-compliance
Lightning Source LLC
LaVergne TN
LVHW092048060526
838201LV00047B/1289